You are the greatest book that ever was or ever will be, the infinite depository of all that is. Until the inner teacher opens, all outside teaching is in vain. It must lead to the opening of the book of the heart to have any value.

—*Swami Vivekananda*

धृतराष्ट्र उवाच
धर्मक्षेत्रे कुरुक्षेत्रे समवेता युयुत्सवः ।
मामकाः पाण्डवाश्चैव किमकुर्वत संजय ॥१॥

संजय उवाच
दृष्ट्वा तु पाण्डवानीकं व्यूढं दुर्योधनस्तदा ।
आचार्यमुपसंगम्य राजा वचनमब्रवीत ॥२॥

पश्यैतां पाण्डुपुत्राणामाचार्य महतीं चमूम् ।
व्यूढां द्रुपदपुत्रेण तव शिष्येण धीमता ॥३॥

अत्र शूरा महेष्वासा भीमार्जुनसमा युधि ।
युयुधानो विराटश्च द्रुपदश्च महारथः ॥४॥

धृष्टकेतुश्चेकितानः काशिराजश्च वीर्यवान् ।
पुरुजित्कुन्तिभोजश्च शैब्यश्च नरपुंगवः ॥५॥

युधामन्युश्च विक्रान्त उत्तमौजाश्च वीर्यवान् ।
सौभद्रो द्रौपदेयाश्च सर्व एव महारथाः ॥६॥

अस्माकं तु विशिष्टा ये तान्निबोध द्विजोत्तम ।
नायका मम सैन्यस्य संज्ञार्थं तान्ब्रवीमि ते ॥७॥

भवान्भीष्मश्च कर्णश्च कृपश्च समितिंजयः ।
अश्वत्थामा विकर्णश्च सौमदत्तिस्तथैव च ॥८॥

अन्ये च बहवः शूरा मदर्थे त्यक्तजीविताः ।

The opening lines of the Bhagavad Gita *in Sanskrit*

Contents ☐

Foreword □

Andrew Harvey

When I was twenty-five I left England and the plush but sterile academic life I was leading there to wander for a year around India. During that year I found myself living in Pondicherry at the ashram of Sri Aurobindo, where, with awe and amazement, I read the *Bhagavad Gita* for the first time, and where I was lucky enough to find in an old ashramite, whom I shall call "Mr. Bannerjee," the ideal first guide to its mysteries. Every morning at dawn for a month Mr. Bannerjee, immaculate, wizened, screechy-voiced, clothed in blazing white, and seated in the lotus position, took me through the Gita in the Sanskrit, translating as he went, with baroque exuberance.

On our first meeting he gazed solemnly at me and said, "There are four things you must not forget when it comes to understanding the Gita. The first is that, although it is considered the spiritual masterpiece of Hinduism, its message is timeless and universal and transcends all religion. Note here too, by the way, that 'Hinduism' is itself a name imposed on a whole slew of different cults and faiths by the Greeks who followed Alexander the Great into India. The essence of all of these philosophies— and of religious life itself—is found in the Gita.

"The second thing you must remember if you are ever to pierce the mystery of this spiritual masterpiece is this: The dialogue it enshrines between the divine avatar Krishna and the soldier Arjuna on the battlefield of Kurukshetra is always taking place within the heart and soul of every human being on the battlefield of this terrible and beautiful world. Each one of us contains the doubting, despairing, potentially brave and illumined human being (Arjuna) and the mystery of Krishna (the eternal Divine Self) hidden behind all the veils of our psyche and mind. What the Gita does is dramatize in the most inspired way imaginable and for all time the full truth of this dialogue and the initiation it can make possible into full human divine life.

"The third thing that will help you approach the Gita's mystery with wisdom is to know that you cannot read it as a 'text' or even as a great and sublime mystical poem only. You must approach it slowly, reverently, bringing to your reading of it the whole range of your inner and outer experience and all of the pressing, disturbing questions of your life and search. Only then will the Gita be able to enter your blood and work its holy magic in the core of your being.

"The fourth and last thing that will open to you the doors of the Gita's splendor is to forget all the academic and religious arguments about which of the different 'yogas' or 'ways of divine union' it celebrates. Different schools bias the interpretation of the text to their own vision. The full truth is that the Gita embodies and celebrates a permanently radical fusion of all the traditional Hindu approaches to the Divine in a vision of what the full human divine being should and must be. These different yogas are in the Gita fused into a vision that combines and transcends them all to offer human beings the richest and most complete way of being and acting in the world with divine truth, wisdom, and effectiveness."

In our last class, four marvelous, wild weeks later, Mr. Bannerjee added a fifth prerequisite for reading the Gita: "Always read the *Bhagavad Gita* as if it had just been written and as if it were referring to what is going on in the world right now. If you do, you will find that its power to initiate and inspire is constantly astounding. The Gita was probably written more than two thousand years ago; each different cycle of world civilization will find in it new truth, expressed with permanently fresh urgency."

Now that I have been graced with the chance to introduce others to this masterpiece, I must take up Mr. Bannerjee's challenge and try to express as succinctly as I can what the Gita is saying to me and other seekers, now, at the beginning of the twenty-first century. Its message, I believe, could not be more urgent, or more relevant to the deepest problems and challenges facing humanity.

I believe that the whole of humanity is now in the thick of a battle whose outcome will determine the fate of the planet. This battle is between those forces of Life that want to see us living in harmony with the creation, inspired by divine love, and so able to re-create our devastated world with the powers of the Divine itself, and the forces of death— of ignorance, pride, and greed—that have brought us to the moment where we have almost destroyed Nature and polluted the world's mind and heart with violence and a materialist vision of humanity. The destiny of this vision is so reductive that it threatens us all with despair and meaninglessness at a moment when hope and resolve are crucial. This tremendous battle is being fought out in every arena of our life—in politics, industry, the arts, the sciences, the universities, the media, and in the depths of all of our psyches.

The signs are not encouraging. We have known about the progressive degradation of the environment for more than twenty years now, but almost nothing significant has been done to counteract it. Two billion people are now living in poverty, yet our addiction to an economic system that thrives on such desolation continues unabated. Much of organized religion continues to be largely divisive, drunk on outmoded visions of exclusive truth, and wedded to a vision of the Divine that obsessively restricts transcendence at this moment when the entire immanent body of God-Nature is in mortal danger. The majority of modern seekers in the so-called New Age who pride themselves on participating in a mystical renaissance are in fact largely trapped in a narcissistic coma, apolitical, unconcerned by and blind to the approaching potentially terminal tragedy of the destruction of nature.

Despair, however, is a luxury those who are growing awake in this darkness cannot afford; all those who see the extent of the potential danger and tragedy threatening humanity and nature are compelled to respond with the deepest of themselves. In the *Bhagavad Gita*, those who long to know how to fight wisely for the future will find a handbook of spiritual warriorhood and divine realization that will constantly inspire and ennoble them and infuse them with divine truth and sacred passion.

It is clear, I think, to anyone who sees the depth of the global predicament we are in that there can only be one way out now—the way out of "mystical activism." An activism that is not fed by mystical wisdom and stamina will wither in the fire of persistent and persistently exhausting disappointment and defeat and tend to create as many new problems as those it tries to solve. A mysticism that is not committed to action within the world on behalf of the poor, of the oppressed, and of nature itself condemns itself to futility at a moment when so much is at stake. Only the highest spiritual wisdom and tireless sacred passion for all of life united with pragmatic, radical action on all possible fronts can now help us preserve the planet. The Gita can guide us to this all-transforming fusion of vision and action because, with the Gospels, it is the most wise and challenging celebration of it.

This, then, in plain language, is what I believe is our "inner Krishna's" message to each of us now, as expressed in the Gita: First of all, like Arjuna, face the truth of the battle that rages on all sides in the world; do not indulge in despair, and claim your own spiritual warriorhood.

Second, realize as quickly and as completely as possible your divine identity and origin through whatever way of divine union your temperament opens up to you—whether it is of knowledge or of devotion. Only such an experience of the Divine in and as you will give you the calm, fearlessness, strength, and detachment you will need to be focused, effective, and undeterred.

Third, understand fully and finally the necessity of surrendering your will and the fruit of your actions wholly to the Divine. There are two reasons why this is essential. Total surrender of your will and actions will enable the Divine to use both for its own transforming purposes without the interference of your false self and its mind-concocted agendas. It will also give you direct access to the Divine's own timeless resources of inner peace and inexhaustible sacred passion, which will enable you to stay true to your purpose and your mission whatever defeats or disappointments happen along the way. Through this surrender to God of your will and of the fruits of your actions, become a poised and perfect instrument of the Divine's own sacred plan for humanity, and whatever you do will be the Divine acting in you and through you—thus, far more useful and transformative than any other form of action, however well intentioned or "inspired."

Fourth, when you have really absorbed the lessons of this wisdom of surrender, understand with your whole being that it is not in the end austere or harsh. In fact, it will open to you, as the last wonderful pages of the Gita reveal, a final mystery of divine love that will fill your whole being with a permanent sober ecstasy—an ecstasy that arises from the awareness that you and all beings are loved by God with deathless and unconditional love. And this ecstasy will unveil to you and in you the fullness of your divine humanity.

If you fuse knowledge of your transcendent origin with tireless service in and for God in the ways the Gita makes plain to you, you will come, on earth and in this body, to know divine bliss and be fed by the ceaseless passion-energy of divine love. Human and divine, inner peace and outer action, knowledge and love, will be married in you at ever-greater depths to make you an ever more powerful and radiant warrior for Love and Justice in all dimensions.

The message of the Gita is one of perfect spiritual balance. It challenges fundamentally both those materialist visions that think of humanity and the universe in purely scientific or practical terms and those religious visions of the Divine that see the world as imperfect or merely an illusion. If we listen to this message both in its complexity and in its urgency, we will come to the wonder, bliss, and empowerment of Arjuna himself at the end of this "Song of God." And with more and more of us empowered in this calm and glorious way, the future of our world will, at last, be in wise hands.

I dedicate this introduction to my friend and spiritual warrior, Clarissa Pinkola Estes.

About the Bhagavad Gita □

The best-loved of all Indian scriptures is the *Bhagavad Gita*—often called simply the Gita ("song"). In English its title might be rendered as "Song of the Blessed One" or "Song of the Adorable One." The Adorable One is Lord Krishna, who is God in human form, and the Song is his teaching to humanity.

What the Gita Is About

The teaching of the Gita emerges from a battlefield conversation between Lord Krishna and the warrior-prince Arjuna. The war—which is said to have taken place in India about five thousand years ago—is between two royal families, the Kauravas ("descendants of Kuru") and the Pandavas ("sons of Pandu"). The long story of how this conflict came about is told in the *Mahabharata*, India's vast national epic, of which the *Bhagavad Gita* is the sixth chapter.

The Kauravas are the "bad guys," who deprived their cousins the Pandavas of their rightful kingdom. The Pandavas enter the fight only after their efforts at compromise have failed. Even Krishna—a cousin of the Pandava princes—could not make peace with the evil Kauravas. Krishna would not fight, but he offered Duryodhana, chief of the Kaurava army, a choice between his presence and his army. Duryodhana chose the army, so Krishna granted his presence to the Pandavas by serving as Arjuna's charioteer.

The narrative opens with the blind king Dhritarashtra (father of one hundred sons, the Kauravas), in his palace, asking his minister Sanjaya to tell him about the battle. Through supernatural perception (granted by

Vyasa, the author of the *Mahabharata,* who also appears in the epic as a grandfather of the Pandavas), Sanjaya describes the scene taking place on the distant battlefield. As fighting is about to begin, Arjuna asks Krishna to draw up their chariot between the two armies so that he may survey them. As he views his opponents, Arjuna is suddenly overcome with despair at the prospect of killing his own relatives, friends, and mentors. Realizing the terrible consequences of war, the great archer casts down his bow and arrow, unwilling to fight. The rest of the Gita is Krishna's teaching in response to Arjuna's anguish.

After the *Bhagavad Gita* is concluded, the *Mahabharata* goes on to tell how Krishna leads the Pandavas to victory in a battle between divine and demonic forces that lasts for eighteen days. Krishna as the divine incarnation, or Avatar, has succeeded in rekindling the torch of Love and Truth on the eve of a new world-age—the degenerate period known as the *kali yuga* in which we find ourselves today.

Who Wrote the Gita?

According to Hindu tradition, the author of the *Mahabharata* (including the Gita) was the sage Vyasa, whose name means "compiler." He is said to have also compiled the Vedas, ancient texts based on revelations received by various seers (*rishis*) while in a superconscious state. Thus, although the Gita is officially classed among the texts known as "traditions" (*smriti,* "remembered" knowledge), it has attained the status of a divine revelation (*shruti,* "heard" knowledge that is eternally existent), similar to the Vedas. The Gita is sometimes also called an Upanishad, the term used for mystical writings that convey the "hidden meaning" of the Vedas concerning the true goal of life and how to attain it. If the Upanishads are the cream of the milk of the Vedas, then the Gita is said to be the butter churned from the cream. The philosophy based on the Upanishads is known as Vedanta, and the *Bhagavad Gita* has been deemed "the best authority on Vedanta."

Contemporary secular scholars consider Vyasa to be a legendary figure and not the literal author of the Gita. They date the composition of the

Mahabharata to sometime between the fifth and second centuries BCE and believe that the Gita was added to the epic at a later time. To account for apparent discrepancies in the text, such scholars attribute the *Mahabharata* to several different authors. In terms of chronology, one ordinary human being could not have literally written both the Vedas and the *Mahabharata*. Tradition nonetheless regards Vyasa as a single individual, although not an ordinary human being. According to some authorities, the name of a *rishi* designates not only a specific individual but also a characteristic state of consciousness, along with its functions, which is shared by different historical figures who may bear the same name in the literature. Regarded in this light, the attribution of the *Bhagavad Gita* to Vyasa is more understandable.

The Language of the Gita

The *Bhagavad Gita* has been translated into all the major languages of the world—as well as some minor ones, including Yiddish. The original text was written in Sanskrit, the ancient language of India in which the Hindu scriptures and a vast body of poetry and literature were composed. Technically a "dead" language, Sanskrit is currently spoken only by Vedic scholars, known as pandits, and a small group of revivalists. It is, however, the ancestor of modern Indian languages and an older relative of most modern Western languages as well.

Sanskrit is regarded as a sacred language, and its sound is held to have a powerful transforming effect. The Gita is usually recited as a chant, and listening to a recitation of it in Sanskrit is considered uplifting even if one doesn't understand the words. (A recommended recording of such recitation is included in "Suggested Readings and Resources.")

An unrhymed poem, the Gita is mostly in what is called the *shloka* meter, consisting of four lines of eight syllables each—the translator Winthrop Sargeant compares it to the meter of Longfellow's *Hiawatha* ("By the shores of Gitchee Gumee". . .). A number of stanzas are in the *tristubh* meter, consisting of four lines of eleven syllables each, used during dramatic moments (for example, Arjuna's exclamation upon beholding Krishna's cosmic form, in chapter 11, verses 15–50).

Interpreting the Gita

Numerous pandits and gurus as well as Western scholars have written commentaries on the Gita. The various interpretations do not always agree, and there are many points of controversy. Does the Gita teach monism, monotheism, or dualism? Does it favor the dualistic Samkhya philosophy or the nondualistic Vedanta? The path of knowledge or the path of devotion? Action or inaction? Theism, pantheism, or panentheism? The teaching that the world is real or illusory? Arguments have been made for all of these competing perspectives. A traditional view holds that they are not disagreeing but rather looking at different facets of the same gem. As the Vedas state, truth is ever the same, though the wise speak of it in various ways.

Despite the controversies, most readers can agree that the heart of the Gita's message is "Love God." Perhaps the Gita is best read intuitively rather than analytically. The great modern sage Sri Aurobindo advises us not to be overly concerned with how the Gita was understood in its own place and time; rather we should extract from it the living truths that meet our own spiritual needs, for the Gita's spirit is large, profound, universal, and timeless. As stated in the *Encyclopedia of Religion*, the text "changes with each reader, fluctuates in meaning with each successive generation of interpreters, which is to say, it lives. This vitality constitutes its sacrality."

Krishna as God in Human Form

An important feature of the Gita's teaching is Krishna's identity as the Avatar (from Sanskrit *avatara,* "descent"). The Avatar, who is God directly "descended" into human form (as contrasted with a human being who "ascends" to a state of God-consciousness), appears on earth periodically—in different forms, under different names, in different parts of the world—to restore truth in the world and to shower grace on the lovers of God. In the Vedic tradition, Krishna is worshiped as an Avatar of Vishnu, that aspect of the one indivisible God which preserves and protects the creation. Yet many people regard him as a universal savior comparable to (or even identical with) such world teachers as Christ and Buddha.

The Gita makes clear that Krishna is the Supreme Deity and not simply "a god." This does not mean, however, that only the advent of God as Krishna is worthy of worship, or that any one divine incarnation is superior to any other: all God-realized beings are one in consciousness, because God is always one and the same. As Aurobindo writes, the Avatar, "though he is manifest in the name and form of Krishna, lays no exclusiveness on this one form of his human birth, but on that which it represents, the Divine, the Purushottama [Supreme Spirit], of whom all Avatars are the human births."

Although the name Krishna is usually translated as "Black" or "Dark Blue," some translators give the meaning as "Puller," because Krishna draws the hearts of all beings to himself. Stories about Krishna in the collections of legends known as the Puranas celebrate his irresistibly loving and lovable nature—as a mischievous child and youth, playing his enchanting flute and attracting the devotion of the cowherding girls and boys (for Krishna himself was chief of the cowherds). Swami Nikhilananda writes: "No eyes ever had enough of the exquisite beauty of Krishna, the dark-blue form clad in a yellow robe, a garland of wild flowers hanging from His neck, and a peacock feather adorning His crest." This playful and adorable aspect of Krishna is less obvious in the Gita, where attention is drawn more to his role as wise teacher and compassionate friend.

Many writers treat Krishna as a figure of mythology and question whether such a historical personage ever existed; or else they say he was a human hero who was later divinized. A similar controversy is taking place about the historical Jesus versus the mythic Christ. In both cases—and especially in Krishna's, since his advent was so long ago—it is not possible to establish the facts in terms of contemporary methodology. History and legend are now bound too closely to untangle. On the other hand, just as Christian tradition holds that the Gospel accounts were inspired by the Holy Spirit and are not merely the product of their human authors, so too, according to the Vedic tradition, the testimonials of the seers regarding Krishna's advent are based on mystical knowledge that is not merely a fanciful exaggeration of facts but rather a deeper insight into reality arising from advanced states of consciousness.

Aurobindo comments that to the spiritual aspirant, controversies over historicity are a waste of time: the Krishna who matters to us is the eternal incarnation of the Divine that we know by inner experience, not the historical teacher and leader. For his lovers, Lord Krishna is a living reality whose companionship is possible to experience here and now, as devotees of all times (including our own) will attest. The Divine Beloved is always with us and within us, because God *is* our own Self. The Avatar is like the sun, which never actually disappears, even though from our limited perspective it appears to vanish at sunset. This divine presence can be felt when one reads the Gita with a spirit of devotion.

For many people in the world, not only Hindus, reading or reciting a portion of the *Bhagavad Gita* is part of their daily spiritual practice. The hearts of many others have been touched by reading it only once with openness to the transforming power of the words of Lord Krishna. May you be so blessed.

About the Translation and Annotation □

Shri Purohit Swami's 1935 elegant prose version of the *Bhagavad Gita* is a good choice for first-time readers of the text. The translator uses few foreign terms and omits most of the epithets of Krishna and Arjuna sprinkled throughout the dialogue. This approach makes the translation easier to read, since one doesn't have to puzzle over unfamiliar words. Today's readers, however, often want to understand shades of meaning where there are no exact English equivalents. I have therefore provided some of the original Sanskrit wording (with simple, nontechnical spelling rather than the scholarly transliteration seen in other books) and definitions in the annotations. A list of special terms at the back of the book will enable the reader to find definitions for key concepts.

Many readers of spiritual works appreciate inclusive language that avoids the generic use of masculine nouns and pronouns. I have not seen any Gita version or commentary that overcomes this problem or even tries to. Since I wanted to maintain the integrity of Purohit Swami's translation as much as possible, I changed this kind of wording only in a very few instances. I don't believe that the Gita itself is "sexist." Like other great teachings, it is addressed to the understanding of a particular time and place, yet its meaning is universal. The essential message speaks to each of us today, although we may have to look more deeply than the specific historical and religious details of the text to receive it.

I took the liberty of substituting modern language for the thee's and thou's, and changing points of grammar and style such as spelling, capitalization, and punctuation. I altered some of the chapter titles and deleted the "colophons," or closing lines of chapters, omitted from many other editions as well. (As an example, the colophon for chapter 1 reads:

"Thus, in the Holy Book the *Bhagavad Gita*, one of the Upanishads, in the Science of the Supreme Spirit, in the Art of Self-Knowledge, in the colloquy between the Divine Lord Shri Krishna and the Prince Arjuna, stands the first chapter, entitled: The Despondency of Arjuna.")

Quoted passages in the annotations are cited simply by indicating the author's name. To find the exact source of a quotation, please see the "Notes" in the back of the book, keyed to chapter and annotation number. "Suggested Readings and Resources" includes some information about the main commentators quoted.

With the annotations, I sought to make the text more accessible, to point out interesting ideas, to highlight notable interpretations, and to magnify the inspirational value of the Gita. In choosing quotations from well-known commentators, I leaned toward the devotional rather than the scholarly, the practical rather than the theoretical, the symbolic rather than the literal, and the traditional but not the conventionally religious. My intention was not to insist on particular interpretations but to spark interest for further study and contemplation.

I have compiled the annotations as a student of the Gita and a lover of God rather than as a commentator in the traditional sense or as a contributor to modern scholarship. The book demonstrates, I hope, how someone like myself, unschooled in Sanskrit and the Vedic literature, is able to approach this ancient wisdom as a matter of practical spirituality. The primary appeal of the Gita is, after all, to the ordinary seeker rather than the monk or scholar; for the Avatar comes to redeem all of humanity, and his perennial message—"Become one with God through love"—is likewise for everyone.

Bhagavad Gita

1 The Gita begins with the words *Dharmakshetre Kurukshetre,* "on the sacred battlefield of Kurukshetra." *Kshetra* means "field." *Dharma* (literally, "that which sustains or upholds") has several meanings: "the inner code of life; moral, religious, and spiritual law; living faith in God's existence and in one's own existence; soulful duty, especially enjoined by the scriptures; devoted observances of any caste or sect; willingness to abide by the dictates of one's soul" (Chinmoy). *Dharma* might be variously translated as "law," "order," "duty," "righteousness," or "virtue."

Kurukshetra, the battlefield of Kuru (ancestor of the Kauravas), is an actual site in India, northwest of Delhi, sacred because holy men practiced spiritual disciplines there from ancient times. But *kshetra* can also be interpreted as the human body, "the locus of the self" (Barbara Stoler Miller). More broadly, Miller says that the Gita is concerned with "the whole field of human experience, the realm of material nature in which the struggle for self-knowledge occurs."

2 Preceptor *(acharya)*: Drona is the military teacher of the sons of both Pandu and Dhritarashtra.

3 Spiritual guides: *dvija,* literally "the twice-born," refers here to brahmins, members of the highest caste. Males of any of the three higher castes are considered to undergo a second birth when initiated into spiritual life with the investiture of the sacred thread. On the meaning of caste, see ch. 18, n. 5.

4 Karna is a son that Arjuna's mother, Kunti, bore before she married Pandu. Although he is thus a brother of the Pandava princes, it happened that he ended up on the Kauravas' side in the war.

1 □ The Despondency of Arjuna

The King Dhritarashtra asked:

1 O Sanjaya! What happened on the sacred battlefield of Kurukshetra,[1] when my people gathered against the Pandavas?

Sanjaya replied:

2 The Prince Duryodhana, when he saw the army of the Pandavas paraded, approached his preceptor[2] Guru Drona and spoke as follows:

3 "Revered Father! Behold this mighty host of the Pandavas, paraded by the son of King Drupada, your wise disciple.

4 "In it are heroes and great bowmen; the equals in battle of Arjuna and Bhima, Yuyudhana, Virata, and Drupada, great soldiers all;

5 "Dhrishtaketu, Chekitana, the valiant King of Benares, Purujit, Kuntibhoja, Shaivya—a master over many;

6 "Yudhamanyu, Uttamauja, Saubhadra, and the sons of Draupadi, famous men.

7 "Further, take note of all those captains who have ranged themselves on our side, O best of spiritual guides![3] the leaders of my army. I will name them for you.

8 "You come first; then Bhishma, Karna,[4] Kripa, great soldiers; Ashvatthama, Vikarna, and the son of Somadatta;

9 "And many others, all ready to die for my sake, all armed, all skilled in war.

5 | This verse is puzzling because "our army" is the Kauravas, which is the larger force, so why would it seem weaker? Perhaps the moral superiority of the Pandavas makes them seem more powerful. Some translators solve the problem by transposing the names so that Bhishma's army becomes the one that is considered stronger or even "unlimited."

6 | The "lion's roar" is a common expression in Sanskrit for a triumphant or confident declaration. The blowing of the conch is a challenge to fight; thus the Kauravas are shown to be the aggressors. Symbolically, the conch means a call to the spiritual life. Just as Krishna's flute calls the heart to love of the Lord, so does his conch summon the soul to courage in the struggle of life.

Yogananda says that this passage refers to the inner experience of meditation: the Kauravas' conches symbolize vibratory noises caused by restless breathing and bodily sensations that disturb the deep stillness of meditation. By contrast, the sounds of the Pandavas' conches (1.14–18) are uplifting vibrations emanating from the subtle energy centers (chakras) in the spine and brain, indicating the meditator's success in withdrawing consciousness from the external world.

7 | In the *Katha Upanishad*, the chariot is a symbol of the body: "Self rides in the chariot of the body, intellect the firm-footed charioteer, discursive mind the reins. Senses are the horses, objects of desire the roads. When Self is joined to body, mind, sense, none but He enjoys" (Purohit & Yeats).

8 | Dharmaraja is another name for Yudhishthira, one of the five Pandavas. The other four are Arjuna, Bhima, Nakula, and Sahadeva.

9 | The monkey king Hanuman, a hero of the epic *Ramayana,* is a model of devoted service to God in His incarnation as Lord Rama.

10 "Yet our army seems the weaker, though commanded by Bhishma; their army seems the stronger, though commanded by Bhima.**5**

11 "Therefore in the rank and file, let all stand firm in their posts, according to battalions; and all you generals about Bhishma."

12 Then to enliven his spirits, the brave Grandfather Bhishma, eldest of the Kuru clan, blew his conch till it sounded like a lion's roar.**6**

13 And immediately all the conches and drums, the trumpets and horns, blared forth in tumultuous uproar.

14 Then seated in their spacious war chariot,**7** yoked with white horses, Lord Shri Krishna and Arjuna sounded their divine shells.

15 Lord Shri Krishna blew His Panchajanya and Arjuna his Devadatta, brave Bhima his renowned shell, Paundra.

16 The King Dharmaraja,**8** the son of Kunti, blew the Anantavijaya, Nakula and Sahadeva, the Sughosha and Manipushpaka respectively.

17 And the Maharaja of Benares, the great archer; Shikhandi, the great soldier; Dhrishtadyumna, Virata, and Satyaki the invincible;

18 And O King! Drupada, the sons of Draupadi, and Saubhadra the great soldier, blew their conches.

19 The tumult rent the hearts of the sons of Dhritarashtra, and violently shook heaven and earth with its echo.

20 Then beholding the sons of Dhritarashtra, drawn up on the battlefield, ready to begin the fight, Arjuna, whose flag bore the Hanuman,**9**

21 Raising his bow, spoke thus to the Lord Shri Krishna: "O Infallible! Lord of the earth! Please draw up my chariot between the two armies,

22 "So that I may observe those who must fight on my side, those who must fight against me;

23 "And gaze over this array of soldiers, eager to please the sinful son of Dhritarashtra."

[@] "Just as the first day of battle started, Arjuna…asked Krishna, his charioteer, to draw up the chariot between the two armies, and the *Bhagavad Gita*—all 2,800 lines of it—was spoken between Krishna and Arjuna. The great Yale Sanskritist Franklin Edgerton has called this a dramatic absurdity. With all due respect, I do not agree. When God speaks, it is not illogical for time to stand still while armies stand frozen in their places."
                                                                    —Winthrop Sargeant

[10] These first words of Lord Krishna may be regarded as His first instructions to Arjuna. According to Maharishi Mahesh Yogi, they have a significance that has been overlooked by commentators who merely portray Arjuna as "a confused mental wreck." At first Arjuna is confident and eager for battle; but as soon as Krishna directs him to behold the assembled warriors, he is overcome by sadness (1.28) and is unable to fight. In the original Sanskrit, Krishna addresses Arjuna as Partha, meaning "son of Pritha"—an epithet for Arjuna's mother (omitted from the present translation). The mention of his mother, says Maharishi, stirs compassion in Arjuna's heart and conflict in his mind. Krishna has thus deliberately placed him in a state of suspension between love and duty, so that he is unable to act. Why did Krishna do this? Because in this state Arjuna is ready to request (2.7) and willingly receive the teaching that Krishna wishes to bestow on him; for wisdom cannot be imparted to a person unless he or she asks for it.

[11] Gandiva is the name of Arjuna's magical bow, with its two inexhaustible quivers and the power of a thousand bows. It was given to him by Agni (god of fire), who got it from Varuna (god of waters), who got it from Soma (god of the ritual *soma* plant, worshiped as a source of creative power). A bow, according to Sri Aurobindo, is a "symbol of the force [*shakti*, power, energy] sent out to reach its mark."

[12] Three worlds: in other words, all the universe. The three worlds can be heaven, earth, and hell; the gross (physical), subtle (mental), and causal (divine) worlds; or the human, semidivine, and divine realms (earth, atmospheric regions, and heavens).

Sanjaya said:

24 Having listened to the request of Arjuna, Lord Shri Krishna drew up His bright chariot exactly in the midst between the two armies,

25 Whither Bhishma and Drona had led all the rulers of the earth, and spoke thus: "O Arjuna! Behold these members of the family of Kuru assembled."**10**

26 There Arjuna noticed fathers, grandfathers, uncles, cousins, sons, grandsons, teachers, friends;

27 Fathers-in-law and benefactors, arrayed on both sides. Arjuna then gazed at all those kinsmen before him.

28 And his heart melted with pity and sadly he spoke: "O my Lord! When I see all these, my own people, thirsting for battle,

29 "My limbs fail me and my throat is parched, my body trembles and my hair stands on end.

30 'The bow Gandiva**11** slips from my hand, and my skin burns. I cannot keep quiet, for my mind is in a tumult.

31 'The omens are adverse; what good can come from the slaughter of my people on this battlefield?

32 "Ah, my Lord! I crave not for victory, nor for kingdom, nor for any pleasure. What were a kingdom or happiness or life to me,

33 "When those for whose sake I desire these things stand here about to sacrifice their property and their lives:

34 "Teachers, fathers, and grandfathers, sons and grandsons, uncles, fathers-in-law, brothers-in-law, and other relatives.

35 "I would not kill them, even for the three worlds;**12** why then for this poor earth? It matters not if I myself am killed.

36 "My Lord! What happiness can come from the death of these sons of Dhritarashtra? We shall sin if we kill these desperate men.

13 The reference is to Hindu rites for the dead ancestors, which may not be performed by children of mixed-caste marriages.

14 "Arjuna has turned a complete pacifist and adopted the policy of non-resistance to evil. But this policy is wrong, inasmuch as if one sees evil one must resist it. The real attitude of non-violence follows from the perception of God in all beings. Only the man whose mind has gone beyond good and evil does not resist evil, for he does not see evil. Further, Arjuna is a kshatriya [member of the warrior caste]; hence it is his duty to fight in a righteous cause" (Nikhilananda).

@ "All life is a battlefield...; whether we like it or not, we are born to fight. We have no choice in this, but we do have the choice of our opponent and our weapon. If we fight other people, often our dear ones, we cannot but lose, but if we choose to fight all that is selfish and violent in us, we cannot but win. There is no such thing as defeat on the spiritual path once we join Sri Krishna, but if we try to fight against him, we shall never know victory." —Eknath Easwaran

37 "We are worthy of a nobler feat than to slaughter our relatives—the sons of Dhritarashtra; for, my Lord! how can we be happy if we kill our kinsmen?

38 "Although these men, blinded by greed, see no guilt in destroying their kin or fighting against their friends,

39 "Should not we, whose eyes are open, who consider it to be wrong to annihilate our house, turn away from so great a crime?

40 "The destruction of our kindred means the destruction of the traditions of our ancient lineage, and when these are lost, irreligion will overrun our homes.

41 "When irreligion spreads, the women of the house begin to stray; when they lose their purity, adulteration of the stock follows.

42 "Promiscuity ruins both the family and those who defile it; while the souls of our ancestors droop, through lack of the funeral cakes and ablutions.[13]

43 "By the destruction of our lineage and the pollution of blood, ancient class traditions and family purity alike perish.

44 "The wise say, my Lord! that they are forever lost, whose ancient traditions are lost.

45 "Alas, it is strange that we should be willing to kill our own countrymen and commit a great sin, in order to enjoy the pleasures of a kingdom.

46 "If, on the contrary, the sons of Dhritarashtra, with weapons in their hands, should slay me, unarmed and unresisting, surely that would be better for my welfare!"

Sanjaya said:

47 Having spoken thus, in the midst of the armies, Arjuna sank on the seat of the chariot, casting away his bow and arrow, heartbroken with grief.[14]

1 "Aryan" derives from the Sanskrit *arya* ("noble" or "honorable"), a word applied in ancient times to great spiritual personalities. Western scholars adopted the term to designate a category of Indo-Iranian languages as well as an ethnic or racial group, also known as "Indo-Europeans." These Aryans were a fair-skinned nomadic people believed to have migrated in prehistoric times from the plains north of the Caucasus, some tribes settling in northern Europe, others in Iran and northern India. The "Aryan invasion" of India has been questioned by authors such as Georg Feuerstein and David Frawley, who argue that the Sanskrit-speaking Vedic Aryans were not foreign invaders but indigenous inhabitants of India. The Nazis promoted the fiction, concocted in Europe in the nineteenth century, of a morally superior "Aryan race," of which Nordic or Germanic peoples were supposedly the purest examples.

2 Effeminacy: The Sanskrit original means "weakness of heart." "In this world which baffles our reason, violence there will always be. The Gita shows the way which will lead us out of it, but it also says that we cannot escape it by running away from it like cowards" (Gandhi).

3 As it happened, so many arrows were shot into Bhishma during the battle that he was able to lie parallel to the ground, supported by the arrow shafts. This event furnished the model for the well-known "bed of nails" used by some Indian ascetics. Bhishma lay on his bed of arrows and waited to die until the sun turned north, thus choosing an auspicious moment for his death in the manner described in 8.24.

2 □ The Philosophy of Discrimination: Samkhya Yoga

1 Sanjaya then told how the Lord Shri Krishna, seeing Arjuna overwhelmed with compassion, his eyes dimmed with flowing tears and full of despondency, consoled him.

The Lord said:

2 My beloved friend! Why yield, just on the eve of battle, to this weakness which does no credit to those who call themselves Aryans,[1] and only brings them infamy and bars against them the gates of heaven?

3 O Arjuna! Why give way to unmanliness? O you who are the terror of your enemies! Shake off such shameful effeminacy,[2] make ready to act!

Arjuna argued:

4 My Lord! How can I, when the battle rages, send an arrow through Bhishma[3] and Drona, who should receive my reverence?

5 Rather would I content myself with a beggar's crust than kill these teachers of mine, these precious noble souls! To slay these masters who are my benefactors would be to stain the sweetness of life's pleasure with their blood.

6 Nor can I say whether it were better that they conquer me or for me to conquer them, since I would no longer care to live if I killed these sons of Dhritarashtra, now preparing for fight.

7 My heart is oppressed with pity, and my mind confused as to what my duty is. Therefore, my Lord! tell me what is best for my spiritual welfare; for I am Your disciple. Please direct me, I pray.

11

4 | Lord of All Hearts: This epithet evokes the adorable aspect of Krishna, who, in his youth as a cowherd in the village of Brindaban, won the hearts of the cowherding girls *(gopis)* and boys *(gopas)*. Krishna is often called Govinda, meaning chief of the cowherds, which reflects his mastery of the senses (symbolized by cows).

5 | Krishna's smile has been interpreted in several different ways. Some commentators think that Krishna is mocking Arjuna with his smile, but if we realize that Krishna, as a spiritual teacher, has only Arjuna's welfare at heart, we may envision the smile as an expression of grace, affection, or patient encouragement. Maharishi points out that although Arjuna is in despair, the Lord smiles in his usual playful mood to show Arjuna that his difficulties are not so serious as he thinks. Yogananda interprets the entire Gita as symbolic of internal experiences of the practitioner of yoga who is battling inner obstacles to liberation. He thus offers the image of Arjuna "basking in the illumining smile of Spirit" as he begins to receive Krishna's sublime discourse.

6 | "Life is a series of experiences which need innumerable forms. Death is an interval in that one long life" (Meher Baba).

7 | "Krishna is not speaking of the Stoic calmness, in which agitation of feeling is not outwardly expressed. The calmness of which He speaks is based on the knowledge of the Soul's immortality" (Nikhilananda).

8 | "That which is not" is the ever-changing Nature (Prakriti); "that which is" is the eternal Spirit (Purusha in the Samkhya philosophy) or Self (Atman in Vedanta). "The ocean can exist without the waves, but the waves cannot manifest without the ocean. The ocean is the real substance, the waves are only temporary changes on the ocean, and therefore 'unreal' (in themselves they have no independent existence). The ocean, in essence, does not change whether it is calm or restless with waves; but the waves change their forms—they come and they go. Their essence is change, and therefore unreality" (Yogananda).

8 For should I attain the monarchy of the visible world, or over the invisible world, it would not drive away the anguish which is now paralyzing my senses.

Sanjaya continued:

9 Arjuna, the conqueror of all enemies, then told the Lord of All Hearts[4] that he would not fight, and became silent, O King!

10 Thereupon the Lord, with a gracious smile,[5] addressed him who was so much depressed in the midst between the two armies.

Lord Shri Krishna said:

11 Why grieve for those for whom no grief is due, and yet profess wisdom? The wise grieve neither for the dead nor for the living.

12 There was never a time when I was not, nor you, nor these princes were not; there will never be a time when we shall cease to be.

13 As the soul experiences in this body, infancy, youth, and old age, so finally it passes into another.[6] The wise have no delusion about this.

14 Those external relations which bring cold and heat, pain and happiness, they come and go; they are not permanent. Endure them bravely, O Prince!

15 The hero whose soul is unmoved by circumstance, who accepts pleasure and pain with equanimity,[7] only he is fit for immortality.

16 That which is not, shall never be; that which is, shall never cease to be.[8] To the wise, these truths are self-evident.

17 The Spirit, which pervades all that we see, is imperishable. Nothing can destroy the Spirit.

18 The material bodies which this Eternal, Indestructible, Immeasurable Spirit inhabits are all finite. Therefore fight, O Valiant Man!

19 He who thinks that the Spirit kills, and he who thinks of it as killed,

9 Verses 2.19–20 are quoted from the *Katha Upanishad* (1.2.19 and 1.2.18, respectively).

10 "He who is afraid kills. He for whom there is no death will not kill" (Gandhi).

11 Soldier: kshatriya, the caste of warriors and rulers. A righteous war is welcome because the duty *(svadharma)* of the soldier is to uphold justice and protect the people. For more on duty, see ch. 3, n. 10; on caste, see ch. 18, n. 5.

are both ignorant. The Spirit kills not, nor is it killed.

20 It was not born; It will never die: nor once having been, can It ever cease to be: Unborn, Eternal, Ever-enduring, yet Most Ancient, the Spirit dies not when the body is dead.[9]

21 He who knows the Spirit as Indestructible, Immortal, Unborn, Always-the-Same, how should he kill or cause to be killed?[10]

22 As a man discards his threadbare robes and puts on new, so the Spirit throws off Its worn-out bodies and takes fresh ones.

23 Weapons cleave It not, fire burns It not, water drenches It not, and wind dries It not.

24 It is impenetrable; It can be neither drowned nor scorched nor dried. It is Eternal, All-pervading, Unchanging, Immovable, and Most Ancient.

25 It is named the Unmanifest, the Unthinkable, the Immutable. Wherefore, knowing the Spirit as such, you have no cause to grieve.

26 Even if you think of it as constantly being born, constantly dying; even then, O Mighty Man! you still have no cause to grieve.

27 For death is as sure for that which is born as birth is for that which is dead. Therefore grieve not for what is inevitable.

28 The end and beginning of beings are unknown. We see only the intervening formations. Then what cause is there for grief?

29 One hears of the Spirit with surprise, another thinks It marvelous, the third listens without comprehending. Thus, though many are told about It, scarcely is there one who knows It.

30 Be not anxious about these armies. The Spirit in man is imperishable.

31 You must look at your duty. Nothing can be more welcome to a soldier than a righteous war.[11] Therefore to waver in your resolve is unworthy, O Arjuna!

12 Kunti is the mother of three of the five Pandava princes—Arjuna, Yudhishthira, and Bhima. (She is also Krishna's aunt.) Krishna often addresses Arjuna as Kaunteya, "son of Kunti." Since her sons are all great heroes, Krishna seems to be reminding Arjuna of his heroic status.

@ "The Gita is not a justification of war, nor does it propound a war-making mystique…. The Gita is saying that even in what appears 'unspiritual,' one can act with pure intentions and thus be guided by Krishna consciousness." —Thomas Merton

13 The "philosophy of Knowledge" is Samkhya, one of six traditional systems of Indian philosophy; elsewhere it is referred to as *jnana yoga*. Among its teachings is the distinction between soul and body explained by Krishna above. It also stresses renunciation of action.

14 The "philosophy of Action" is Yoga, specifically *karma yoga*, which stresses renunciation of the fruits of action but not of action itself.

@ The various schools of philosophy need not be seen as competing with one another: "Sankhya and Yoga are never at daggers drawn. One is detached meditative knowledge, and the other is dedicated and selfless action. They have the self-same Goal. They just follow two different paths to arrive at the Goal." —Sri Chinmoy

15 Figurative: literally "flowery." The ignorant are attached to words and think there is nothing in the Vedas but rituals for attaining heaven, wealth, and the like; they ignore the teachings that lead to liberation.

32 Blessed are the soldiers who find their opportunity. This opportunity has opened for you the gates of heaven.

33 Refuse to fight in this righteous cause, and you will be a traitor, lost to fame, incurring only sin.

34 Men will talk forever of your disgrace; and to the noble, dishonor is worse than death.

35 Great generals will think that you have fled from the battlefield through cowardice; though once honored, you will seem despicable.

36 Your enemies will spread scandal and mock at your courage. Can anything be more humiliating?

37 If killed, you shall attain heaven; if victorious, enjoy the kingdom of earth. Therefore arise, O son of Kunti!**12** and fight.

38 Look upon pleasure and pain, victory and defeat, with an equal eye. Make ready for the combat, and you shall commit no sin.

39 I have told you the philosophy of Knowledge.**13** Now listen! and I will explain the philosophy of Action,**14** by means of which, O Arjuna, you shall break through the bondage of all action.

40 On this Path, endeavor is never wasted, nor can it ever be repressed. Even a very little of its practice protects one from great danger.

41 By its means, the straying intellect becomes steadied in the contemplation of one object only; whereas the minds of the irresolute stray into bypaths innumerable.

42 Only the ignorant speak in figurative**15** language. It is they who extol the letter of the scriptures, saying, "There is nothing deeper than this."

43 Consulting only their desires, they construct their own heaven, devising arduous and complex rites to secure their own pleasure and their own power; and the only result is rebirth.

16 Vedic Scriptures: *Rig Veda* (verses and songs in praise of the gods), *Sama Veda* (chants), *Yajur Veda* (a priestly manual for performing rituals of sacrifice), and *Atharva Veda* (magic formulas).

17 In Sanskrit, the first of the three Qualities *(gunas)* is *sattva,* called Purity in this version (other translators render it as goodness, consciousness, or truth). *Rajas* is Passion (desire, attachment, activity, the dynamic principle), and *tamas* is Ignorance (inertia, darkness).

The doctrine of the three Qualities is found in the Vedas, which prescribe rituals for those who, under the influence of the Qualities, seek to attain material rewards and blessings of the gods. Such rituals are the very opposite of what Krishna is teaching about action without concern for reward. So, in telling Arjuna to rise above the Qualities, Krishna seems also to say that the spiritual seeker ultimately has to go beyond the conventions of rites, rituals, and scriptures.

18 Other translators interpret this verse to mean that an enlightened person has no need for scriptures, just as there is no need for a well when the whole countryside is flooded. "The state of realization is like a reservoir full of water, from which people quite naturally draw to satisfy all their needs instead of getting their water from many small ponds. Therefore the Lord asks Arjuna to 'be without the three gunas' and not waste his life in planning and achieving small gains in the ever-changing field of the three gunas" (Maharishi).

19 Pure Intelligence: *buddhi yoga,* "taking refuge in the 'wisdom-faculty'" (Feuerstein). On *buddhi,* see below, n. 27.

20 Contemplation of the Infinite: *samadhi,* a state of consciousness equated with ecstatic concentration on the object of meditation, so that all mental activity stops.

21 "Spirituality" is Purohit Swami's translation of the word *yoga,* which signifies the state of union with God as well as any of several paths or disciplines that lead to union. The physical discipline known as *hatha yoga* is the best-known yoga in the West, but many regard it as only a preliminary path leading to more advanced practices.

44 While their minds are absorbed with ideas of power and personal enjoyment, they cannot concentrate their discrimination on one point.

45 The Vedic Scriptures[16] tell of the three constituents of life—the Qualities.[17] Rise above all of them, O Arjuna! above all the pairs of opposing sensations; be steady in truth, free from worldly anxieties, and centered in the Self.

46 As a man can drink water from any side of a full tank, so the skilled theologian can wrest from any scripture that which will serve his purpose.[18]

47 But you have only the right to work; but none to the fruit thereof. Let not then the fruit of your action be your motive; nor yet be enamored of inaction.

48 Perform all your actions with mind concentrated on the Divine, renouncing attachment and looking upon success and failure with an equal eye. Spirituality implies equanimity.

49 Physical action is far inferior to an intellect concentrated on the Divine. Have recourse then to the Pure Intelligence.[19] It is only the petty-minded who work for reward.

50 When a man attains to Pure Reason, he renounces in this world the results of good and evil alike. Cling to Right Action. Spirituality is the real art of living.

51 The sages guided by Pure Intellect renounce the fruit of action; and, freed from the chains of rebirth, they reach the highest bliss.

52 When your reason has crossed the entanglements of illusion, then shall you become indifferent both to the philosophies you have heard and to those you may yet hear.

53 When the intellect, bewildered by the multiplicity of holy scripts, stands unperturbed in blissful contemplation of the Infinite,[20] then have you attained Spirituality.[21]

22 "This question of Arjuna's introduces the glorious eighteen stanzas [2.55–72] which, as Gandhi points out, hold the key to the interpretation of the entire *Bhagavad Gita*. Gandhi, a devoted student of the Gita, was especially drawn to these last eighteen verses of the second chapter…. In every verse of this passage we have clear proof that the battle referred to is within, between the forces of selfishness and the forces of selflessness, between the ferocious pull of the senses and the serene tranquility of spiritual wisdom. I strongly recommend these verses to be memorized for use in meditation because they gradually can bring about the transformation of our consciousness" (Easwaran).

23 Accepts good and evil alike: This means that one does not get over-excited when good things happen or upset when bad things happen. It does not imply that one invites or sanctions evil. As Ramakrishna said, God is in everything—but you do not embrace a tiger.

24 The tortoise image is a favorite metaphor for the practice of *pratya-hara*, withdrawal of the senses or the "ability to free sense activity from the domination of external objects" (Eliade). "The senses can be involved with outer experiences and yet not be totally engrossed in them to the extent that they transfer to the mind impressions deep enough to become the seed of future desires" (Maharishi).

25 Mind: *manas*, here meaning the lower mind, which receives impressions from the senses and relays them to the higher mind (*buddhi*; see n. 27). The function of *manas* includes both thought and emotion.

26 Desire *(kama)* is said to breed anger because anger arises when desire is thwarted.

27 Reason: *buddhi*, rendered elsewhere as "intelligence" or "intellect," the seat of wisdom *(jnana, vidya, prajna)*. The word comes from the root *bud*, "to awaken." "Buddhi is the aspect of consciousness that is filled with light and reveals the truth. When one's Buddhi becomes fully developed, one becomes a Buddha, or enlightened one. The main action of intelligence is to discern the true and real from the false and unreal" (Frawley).

Arjuna asked:

54 My Lord! How can we recognize the saint who has attained Pure Intellect, who has reached this state of Bliss, and whose mind is steady? How does he talk, how does he live, and how does he act?[22]

Lord Shri Krishna replied:

55 When a man has given up the desires of his heart and is satisfied with the Self alone, be sure that he has reached the highest state.

56 The sage, whose mind is unruffled in suffering, whose desire is not roused by enjoyment, who is without attachment, anger, or fear—take him to be one who stands at that lofty level.

57 He who, wherever he goes, is attached to no person and to no place by ties of flesh; who accepts good and evil alike,[23] neither welcoming the one nor shrinking from the other—take him to be one who is merged in the Infinite.

58 He who can withdraw his senses from the attraction of their objects, as the tortoise draws his limbs within his shell[24]—take it that such a one has attained Perfection.

59 The objects of sense turn from him who is abstemious. Even the relish for them is lost in him who has seen the Truth.

60 O Arjuna! The mind[25] of him who is trying to conquer it is forcibly carried away in spite of his efforts, by his tumultuous senses.

61 Restraining them all, let him meditate steadfastly on Me; for who thus conquers his senses achieves perfection.

62 When a man dwells on the objects of sense, he creates an attraction for them; attraction develops into desire, and desire breeds anger.[26]

63 Anger induces delusion; delusion, loss of memory; through loss of memory, reason[27] is shattered; and loss of reason leads to destruction.

28 Eternal peace: *prasada*, serenity or clarity. *Prasada* also means "grace." Srila Prabhupada translates it in this verse as "the complete mercy of the Lord." By the grace or mercy of God, the devotee becomes liberated from delusion.

29 Reason: *prajna*. See above, n. 27.

30 Saint: *muni*, "silent one." A *muni* is an advanced aspirant who has reached a high level of consciousness through practicing austerities such as silence. The English word *saint* has specific associations in Christianity. In this translation, a more general sense of spiritual holiness seems to be intended.

31 Self, Supreme Spirit: Brahman, the ultimate Reality, the formless absolute state of God, which is inseparable from the personal God and also identical with the soul or inmost self (Atman) of every being. Brahman is all, the One without a second. Because it cannot be described, it is often referred to by negation: *neti, neti*, "not this, not that."

32 "Become one with the Eternal": literally, "reach the *nirvana* of Brahman." *Nirvana* means "blown out," like a candle, but it is not utter extinction or a state of nonbeing; Sri Easwaran explains it as the extinction of the limited, selfish personality. The illusion of separate individuality ceases to exist when the self merges with Brahman, just as the limited nature of a drop of seawater disappears when it reunites with the ocean.

@ "One of the beauties of the *Bhagavad Gita* is that it does not say 'You should do this' or 'You shouldn't do that.' Sri Krishna simply says that if you want joy, security, wisdom, then this is the path. If you want sorrow, insecurity, and despair, then that is the path. He gives both maps in graphic detail, and tells you that it is for you to decide where you want to go."
　　　　　　　　　　　　　　　　　　　　　　　—Eknath Easwaran

64 But the self-controlled soul, who moves among sense objects free from either attachment or repulsion, he wins eternal peace.[28]

65 Having attained peace, he becomes free from misery; for when the mind gains peace, right discrimination follows.

66 Right discrimination is not for him who cannot concentrate. Without concentration, there cannot be meditation; he who cannot meditate must not expect peace; and without peace, how can anyone expect happiness?

67 As a ship at sea is tossed by the tempest, so the reason[29] is carried away by the mind when preyed upon by the straying senses.

68 Therefore, O Mighty-in-Arms! he who keeps his senses detached from their objects—take it that his reason is purified.

69 The saint[30] is awake when the world sleeps, and he ignores that for which the world lives.

70 He attains peace into whom desires flow as rivers into the ocean, which though brimming with water remains ever the same; not he whom desire carries away.

71 He attains peace who, giving up desire, moves through the world without aspiration, possessing nothing which he can call his own, and free from pride.

72 O Arjuna! This is the state of the Self, the Supreme Spirit,[31] to which if a man once attain, it shall never be taken from him. Even at the time of leaving the body, he will remain firmly enthroned there, and will become one with the Eternal.[32]

1 Freedom from activity: *naishkarmya*, the calm state of "actionless action" enjoyed by those who are without desire. Such persons may not be active in the world, but their very presence helps others. However, *naishkarmya* does not necessarily mean inactivity; it means action free from the binding sense of oneself as the doer. "The objective of spiritual advancement is not so much 'works' but the quality of life free from ego-consciousness" (Meher Baba).

3 □ The Path of Action: Karma Yoga

Arjuna questioned:

1 My Lord! If wisdom is above action, why do you advise me to engage in this terrible fight?

2 Your language perplexes me and confuses my reason. Therefore please tell me the only way by which I may, without doubt, secure my spiritual welfare.

Lord Shri Krishna replied:

3 In this world, as I have said, there is a twofold path, O Sinless One! There is the Path of Wisdom for those who meditate and the Path of Action for those who work.

4 No man can attain freedom from activity[1] by refraining from action, nor can one reach perfection by merely refusing to act.

5 He cannot even for a moment remain really inactive; for the Qualities of Nature will compel him to act whether he will or no.

6 Whoever remains motionless, refusing to act, but all the while brooding over sensuous objects, that deluded soul is simply a hypocrite.

7 But, O Arjuna! All honor to him whose mind controls his senses; for he is thereby beginning to practice Karma Yoga, the Path of Right Action, keeping himself always unattached.

8 Do your duty as prescribed; for action for duty's sake is superior to inaction. Even the maintenance of the body would be impossible if one remained inactive.

2 Sacrifice: *yajna*. Literally, this word refers to ancient Vedic oblations offered to the sacred fire. Its inner meaning is any action done with self-giving love, free from ego-consciousness, with the motive of pleasing the Lord; "an offering of oneself, one's being, one's mind, heart, will, body, life, actions to the Divine" (Aurobindo).

@ "Let us give up our whole body and mind and everything as an eternal sacrifice unto the Lord and be at peace, perfect peace, with ourselves. Instead of pouring oblations into the fire, as in a sacrifice, perform this one great sacrifice day and night—the sacrifice of your little self. 'I searched for wealth in this world; Thou art the only wealth I have found; I sacrifice myself unto Thee. I searched for someone to love; Thou art the only beloved I have found; I sacrifice myself unto Thee.'"   —Swami Vivekananda

3 The entire universe was created from the sacrifice of the gigantic body of the Cosmic Person, known as Purusha or Prajapati (the Creator of *praja*, human beings). The principle of sacrifice thus plays an essential role from the very beginning of life to its ultimate goal, God-Realization. Through *yajna*, life flourishes and bears fruit.

4 Powers of Nature: *devas*, literally "shining ones," often translated as "gods." The *devas* are divine beings equated with the forces of nature and are distinct from the one supreme God. They represent certain "offices" that are filled successively by various souls. But although they may dwell in the heavenly realms, they are neither immortal nor spiritually perfect. Spiritual perfection can only be attained in human form.

9   In this world people are fettered by action, unless it is performed as a sacrifice.[2] Therefore, O Arjuna! let your acts be done without attachment, as sacrifice only.

10 In the beginning, when God created all beings by the sacrifice of Himself, He said unto them: "Through sacrifice you can procreate, and it shall satisfy all your desires.[3]

11 "Worship the Powers of Nature[4] thereby, and let them nourish you in return; thus supporting each other, you shall attain your highest welfare.

12 "For, fed on sacrifice, Nature will give you all the enjoyment you can desire. But whoever enjoys what she gives without returning is, indeed, a robber."

13 The sages who enjoy the food that remains after the sacrifice is made are freed from all sin; but the selfish who spread their feast only for themselves feed on sin only.

14 All creatures are the product of food, food is the product of rain, rain comes by sacrifice, and sacrifice is the noblest form of action.

15 All action originates in the Supreme Spirit, which is Imperishable, and in sacrificial action the all-pervading Spirit is consciously present.

16 Thus he who does not help the revolving wheel of sacrifice, but instead leads a sinful life, rejoicing in the gratification of his senses, O Arjuna! he breathes in vain.

17 On the other hand, the soul who meditates on the Self, is content to serve the Self, and rests satisfied within the Self—there remains nothing more for him to accomplish.

18 He has nothing to gain by the performance or nonperformance of action. His welfare depends not on any contribution that an earthly creature can make.

19 Therefore do your duty perfectly, without care for the results; for he who does his duty disinterestedly attains the Supreme.

5 King Janaka was an enlightened ruler and the father of Sita, heroine of the epic *Ramayana*. He continued to be active in the world even after attaining perfection, for the sake of "enlightening the world": *loka-samgraha*. This famous phrase from the Gita literally means "world gathering" or harmonizing the world. To help others toward enlightenment is the highest form of selfless service. The ideal of *loka-samgraha* is the basis of the Mahayana Buddhist path of the bodhisattva.

6 Personal egotism: *ahamkara*, the consciousness of "I." The activity of this organ of self-consciousness creates the illusion of the self as separate from God and causes us to identify ourselves as the agent of action. Ramana Maharshi (1879–1950) taught meditation on the question "Who am I?" as a means of uprooting this identification with the false ego.

@ "There are two types of ego. The false ego has innumerable wants and desires. It says, I am a man, I want this; I am a woman, I want that; I am sick; I want to be happy; I am rich; I am very poor.... It is always 'I.' But when this ego is annihilated, a transformation takes place: the false 'I' is replaced by the real 'I,' and the experience, 'I am free from desires and wanting, I am infinite, I am one with God,' is gained. That is the Real Ego." —Meher Baba

7 "This injunction of the Gita does not mean that a saint should not awaken people at all; they should be gradually roused, and instructed in higher principles only when they are receptive—when they begin to wonder about the mysteries of life, either as a result of introspective thinking or of worldly misfortune and material disillusionment" (Yogananda).

8 Surrendering: that is, dedicating one's every action to God and leaving to him the responsibility for its results.

9 Bondage of all action: a reference to the natural law of karma (Sanskrit *karman*). By this law, whatever we are and whatever we do is the consequence of impressions *(samskaras)* deposited in the mental body by our thoughts, words, and deeds of past lives. These impressions,

20 King Janaka[5] and others attained perfection through action alone. Even for the sake of enlightening the world, it is your duty to act;

21 For whatever a great man does, others imitate. People conform to the standard which he has set.

22 There is nothing in this universe, O Arjuna! that I am compelled to do; nor anything for Me to attain; yet I am persistently active.

23 For were I not to act without ceasing, O Prince! people would be glad to do likewise.

24 And if I were to refrain from action, the human race would be ruined; I should lead the world to chaos, and destruction would follow.

25 As the ignorant act because of their fondness for action, so should the wise act without such attachment, fixing their eyes, O Arjuna! only on the welfare of the world.

26 But a wise man should not perturb the minds of the ignorant, who are attached to action; let him perform his own actions in the right spirit, with concentration on Me, thus inspiring all to do the same.

27 Action is the product of the Qualities inherent in Nature. It is only the ignorant man who, misled by personal egotism,[6] says: "I am the doer."

28 But he, O Mighty One! who understands correctly the relation of the Qualities to action is not attached to the act, for he perceives that it is merely the action and reaction of the Qualities among themselves.

29 Those who do not understand the Qualities are interested in the act. Still, the wise man who knows the truth should not disturb the mind of him who does not.[7]

30 Therefore, surrendering[8] your actions unto Me, your thoughts concentrated on the Absolute, free from selfishness and without anticipation of reward, with mind devoid of excitement, begin to fight.

31 Those who act always in accordance with My precepts, firm in faith and without caviling, they too are freed from the bondage of action.[9]

carried in latent form into our next life, determine our future temperament and destiny. Just as one can be bound by a chain of gold or a chain of iron, so good as well as bad actions can bind us spiritually. But, as Meher Baba explains: "Good as well as bad karma binds as long as it feeds the ego-mind through wrong understanding. But karma becomes a power for Emancipation when it springs from right understanding and wears out the ego-mind."

10 In one sense, our own duty *(svadharma)* is the activity appropriate to our station in life. Whatever work happens to be our lot in life might be considered our duty. More broadly, it is our life purpose, an ideal to which we are inwardly called. If we follow the path suited to our own nature, we will make good progress; but if we try to imitate someone else's path, we are in danger of falling back. Such a loss would be worse than death, which after all is "only a temporary pause in the process of evolution. A pause like this is no real danger to life because, with a new body taken after the pause, more rapid progress in life evolution becomes possible" (Maharishi). The safest and most effective path, then, is one's own duty, even if performed imperfectly or unsuccessfully—as long as we work honestly, at activities that do not harm others, and leave the results to God.

@ "Any action that makes us go Godward is a good action and is our duty; any action that makes us go downward is evil and is not our duty."

—Swami Vivekananda

11 Wanting pleasure and wishing to avoid pain are two sides of the same coin; both attraction and aversion are born of desire.

12 Mind: *manas*. Reason: *buddhi*.

13 "He" refers here to God, the indwelling Supreme Self. "He, the Self, the witness of reason, is superior to reason" (Shankara).

32 But they who ridicule My word and do not keep it are ignorant, devoid of wisdom, and blind. They seek but their own destruction.

33 Even the wise man acts in character with his nature; indeed, all creatures act according to their natures. What is the use of compulsion then?

34 The love and hate which are aroused by the objects of sense arise from Nature; do not yield to them. They only obstruct the path.

35 It is better to do your own duty,[10] however lacking in merit, than to do that of another, even though efficiently. It is better to die doing one's own duty, for to do the duty of another is fraught with danger.

Arjuna asked:

36 My Lord! Tell me, what is it that drives a man to sin, even against his will and as if by compulsion?

Lord Shri Krishna said:

37 It is desire, it is aversion, born of passion.[11] Desire consumes and corrupts everything. It is man's greatest enemy.

38 As fire is shrouded in smoke, a mirror by dust, and a child by the womb, so is the universe enveloped in desire.

39 It is the wise man's constant enemy; it tarnishes the face of wisdom. It is as insatiable as a flame of fire.

40 It works through the senses, the mind, and the reason,[12] and with their help destroys wisdom and confounds the soul.

41 Therefore, O Arjuna! first control your senses, and then slay desire; for it is full of sin, and is the destroyer of knowledge and of wisdom.

42 It is said that the senses are powerful. But beyond the senses is the mind, beyond mind is intellect, and beyond and greater than intellect is He.[13]

43 Thus, O Mighty-in-Arms! knowing him to be beyond the intellect and, by His help, subduing your personal egotism, kill your enemy, Desire, extremely difficult though it be.

1 Manu was the first man, the father of the human race, and the first king. The name Manu is also given to a series of rulers or lawgivers who are considered to be primal ancestors of humanity. The *Laws of Manu* is a famous ancient text of Hindu law attributed to Manu.

2 This teaching was handed down from ancient times in an orderly lineage and benefited the world through the influence of wise rulers; but it was forgotten with the coming of the dark age (see below, n. 6). "Symbolically, throughout many incarnations the senses are engrossed in and identified with matter, and man thus loses the knowledge of reuniting his soul with Spirit" (Yogananda).

3 Will and power: Maya, the magical power of illusion.

4 Verses 7–8 contain one of the earliest references to the idea of the Avatar in the literature of Hinduism, although the word *avatara* ("descent") itself does not appear in the Gita. All beings are in reality forms of the Divine, but most are unconscious of their true identity, while the Avatar is infinitely conscious and performs the role of savior or redeemer.

5 "The Lord is above love and hate. By destroying wickedness the Lord shows the way of liberation to the wicked" (Nikhilananda).

6 Age: *yuga*. There are four ages: *satya, treta, dvapara,* and *kali yuga* (which are likened to the Greek golden, silver, bronze, and iron ages), during which conditions progressively deteriorate. We are said to be now in the dark, materialistic age of *kali yuga*.

4 □ The Path of Wisdom: Jnana Yoga

Lord Shri Krishna said:

1 This imperishable philosophy I taught to Vivasvat, the founder of the Sun-dynasty; Vivasvat gave it to Manu the Lawgiver,**1** and Manu to King Ikshvaku!

2 The Divine Kings knew it, for it was their tradition. Then, after a long time, at last it was forgotten.**2**

3 It is this same ancient path that I have now revealed to you, since you are My devotee and My friend. It is the supreme secret.

Arjuna asked:

4 My Lord! Vivasvat was born before You; how then can You have revealed it to him?

Lord Shri Krishna replied:

5 I have been born again and again, from time to time; you too, O Arjuna! My births are known to Me, but you know not your own.

6 I have no beginning. Though I am imperishable, as well as Lord of all that exists, yet by My own will and power**3** do I manifest Myself.

7 Whenever spirituality decays and materialism is rampant, then, O Arjuna! I reincarnate Myself.**4**

8 To protect the righteous, to destroy the wicked,**5** and to establish the kingdom of God, I am reborn from age to age.**6**

9 He who realizes the divine truth concerning My birth and life is not

7 Illuminating flame of self-abnegation: *jnana tapas,* "austerity of wisdom." *Tapas* (austerity) is the heat or fire of asceticism or self-denial (through disciplines such as fasting, sexual abstinence, and silence) that burns away the hindrances to realization. Here the reference is to cultivating detachment through knowledge or wisdom *(jnana)* as a form of *tapas.* (See also below, n. 20.)

8 "In this verse, one of the most marvelous in the Gita, the Lord says, with his infinite love, that it does not matter what religion you profess. Be a Christian. Be a Jew. Be a Buddhist. Be a Hindu, Muslim, or Zoroastrian. The important point is to follow faithfully what the Lord reveals through your particular scripture with all your heart and all your mind and all your strength and all your spirit, and you will become united with the Lord of Love" (Easwaran).

9 On the four divisions of society, or castes, see ch. 18, n. 5.

10 Sage: *pandita.* In English usage, "pandit" or "pundit" means someone who is learned or authoritative, and sometimes the term is used in a jocular way (as in "political pundits"); but here a pandit is defined as a true practitioner of *karma yoga.*

born again; and when he leaves his body, he becomes one with Me.

10 Many have merged their existence in Mine, being freed from desire, fear, and anger, filled always with Me, and purified by the illuminating flame of self-abnegation.[7]

11 Howsoever men try to worship Me, so do I welcome them. By whatever path they travel, it leads to Me at last.[8]

12 Those who look for success worship the Powers; and in this world their actions bear immediate fruit.

13 The four divisions of society (the wise, the soldier, the merchant, the laborer)[9] were created by Me, according to the natural distribution of Qualities and instincts. I am the author of them, though I Myself do no action and am changeless.

14 My actions do not fetter Me, nor do I desire anything that they can bring. He who thus realizes Me is not enslaved by action.

15 In the light of this wisdom, our ancestors, who sought deliverance, performed their acts. You should act also, as did our fathers of old.

16 What is action and what is inaction? It is a question which has bewildered the wise. But I will declare unto you the philosophy of action, and knowing it, you shall be free from evil.

17 It is necessary to consider what is right action, what is wrong action, and what is inaction; for mysterious is the law of action.

18 He who can see inaction in action, and action in inaction, is the wisest among men. He is a saint, even though he still acts.

19 The wise call him a sage;[10] for whatever he undertakes is free from the motive of desire, and his deeds are purified by the fire of wisdom.

20 Having surrendered all claim to the results of his actions, always contented and independent, in reality he does nothing, even though he is apparently acting.

11 Mind: *chitta*, variously defined as the field of consciousness and attention; thought and feeling; the repository of *samskaras*, impressions created by our thoughts, words, and deeds.

12 In verses 23–33, sacrifice is shown to include not just traditional religious rituals but also yogic disciplines, restraint of the senses, devotion, study, and other practices. "The saving principle constant in all these variations is to subordinate the lower activities, to diminish the control of desire and replace it by a superior energy, to abandon the purely egoistic enjoyment for that diviner delight which comes by sacrifice, by self-dedication, by self-mastery, by the giving up of one's lower impulses to a greater and higher aim" (Aurobindo).

13 Spirit: Brahman. See ch. 2, n. 31.

14 The first kind of self-control means abstaining from sensory experiences. The second is the "middle way" of moderation, neither extreme asceticism nor indulgence, but rather engaging the senses (in contact with permissible objects) as an offering to the Divine, not for one's own gratification.

15 Vitality: *prana*, primal life force or energy; breath of life.

16 Control of the vital energy is *pranayama*, yogic techniques (such as breathing exercises) aimed at controlling the *prana*. Prana and Apana are the upward and downward currents of *prana* that manifest as inhalation and exhalation. Prana converts the oxygen in incoming breath into the life force; Apana is the downward force that removes waste and impurities from the body.

21 Expecting nothing, his mind and personality[11] controlled, without greed, doing bodily actions only—though he acts, yet he remains untainted.

22 Content with what comes to him without effort of his own, mounting above the pairs of opposites, free from envy, his mind balanced both in success and failure—though he act, yet the consequences do not bind him.

23 He who is without attachment, free, his mind centered in wisdom, his actions, being done as a sacrifice, leave no trace behind.[12]

24 For him, the sacrifice itself is the Spirit;[13] the Spirit and the oblation are one; it is the Spirit itself which is sacrificed in Its own fire, and the man even in action is united with God, since while performing his act, his mind never ceases to be fixed on him.

25 Some sages sacrifice to the Powers; others offer themselves on the altar of the Eternal.

26 Some sacrifice their physical senses in the fire of self-control; others offer up their contact with external objects in the sacrificial fire of their senses.[14]

27 Others again sacrifice their activities and their vitality[15] in the spiritual fire of self-abnegation, kindled by wisdom.

28 And yet others offer as their sacrifice wealth, austerities, and meditation. Monks wedded to their vows renounce their scriptural learning, and even their spiritual powers.

29 There are some who practice control of the vital energy and govern the subtle forces of Prana and Apana, thereby sacrificing their Prana unto Apana, or their Apana unto Prana.[16]

30 Others, controlling their diet, sacrifice their worldly life to the spiritual fire. All understand the principle of sacrifice, and by its means their sins are washed away.

17 Nectar of immortality: *amrita*, "nondeath." See ch. 9, n. 6.

18 Sacrifice of wisdom: sacrifice leading to wisdom *(jnana)*, performed through mental action, as described in 4.24. Sri Easwaran interprets the phrase to mean an offering of wisdom: "The greatest gift we can give the Lord is the sharing of spiritual wisdom with others."

19 A devotee of Sai Baba of Shirdi (died 1918) was reciting this verse while massaging the Master's legs. Sai commented: "The verse tells us how a disciple is to approach his Guru in order to attain Realization. He must completely surrender body, mind, soul and possessions to the Guru. That is the prostration referred to. The enquiry must be a constant quest for Truth, not questions asked out of mere curiosity or for a wrong motive, such as to trap the Guru. The motive must be pure desire for spiritual progress and Realization. Then the service is not mere physical service such as massaging. For it to be effective there must be no idea that you are free to give or withhold service; you must feel that your body no longer belongs to you since you have surrendered it to the Guru and it exists only to do him service." He also said, "Divine knowledge is to be realized, not taught." The Master does not give knowledge but simply removes the veil of ignorance concealing knowledge that is innate.

20 Wisdom *(jnana)* burns up the karmic debts set in motion by the impressions of past thoughts, words, and deeds. Although *jnana* is sometimes translated as "knowledge," it does not refer to intellectual knowing but rather to intuitive understanding. The *jnana yogi* acts by the guidance of discrimination (discerning the true from the false) and intuition (the deepest promptings of the heart), not from the influence of stored-up impressions.

21 Perfect saint: literally, "perfected in yoga."

22 Peace *(shanti):* liberation from the false ego and attachment to the belief in Maya, the ever-changing world of appearances.

31 Tasting the nectar of immortality[17] as the reward of sacrifice, they reach the Eternal. This world is not for those who refuse to sacrifice; much less the other world.

32 In this way other sacrifices too may be undergone for the Spirit's sake. Know that they all depend on action. Knowing this, you shall be free.

33 The sacrifice of wisdom[18] is superior to any material sacrifice, for O Arjuna! the climax of action is always Realization.

34 This shall you learn by prostrating yourself at the Master's feet, by questioning Him, and by serving Him. The wise who have realized the Truth will teach you wisdom.[19]

35 Having known that, you shall never again be confounded; and, O Arjuna! by the power of that wisdom, you shall see all these people, as it were, as your own Self, and therefore as Me.

36 Be you the greatest of all sinners, yet you shall cross over all sin by the ferryboat of wisdom.

37 As the kindled fire consumes the fuel, so, O Arjuna! in the flame of wisdom[20] the embers of action are burnt to ashes.

38 There is nothing in the world so purifying as wisdom; and he who is a perfect saint[21] finds that at last in his own Self.

39 He who is full of faith attains wisdom, and he too who can control his senses. Having attained that wisdom, he shall ere long attain the Supreme Peace.[22]

40 But the ignorant man, and he who has no faith, and the skeptic are lost. Neither in this world nor elsewhere is there any happiness in store for him who always doubts.

41 But the man who has renounced his action for meditation, who has cleft his doubt in twain by the sword of wisdom, who remains always enthroned in his Self, is not bound by his acts.

[@] "As the sharp edge of the sword is capable of cutting whatever it meets, so the state of knowledge, the awareness of Being as separate from activity, cuts asunder all doubts about the true nature of life and activity. Until this knowledge dawns, doubts are certain to remain."

—Maharishi Mahesh Yogi

42 Therefore, cleaving asunder with the sword of wisdom the doubts of your heart, which your own ignorance has engendered, follow the Path of Wisdom and arise!

[1] Ascetic: *samnyasin*, renouncer. The *samnyasins* of various Hindu sects break all ties with social customs and institutions, abandon wordly possessions and comforts, shave their heads and go naked or wear ocher garments, and wander from place to place, begging for their food. The Gita contrasts the true *samnyasin* with those who merely follow this external lifestyle while remaining attached to their likes and dislikes.

[2] Wisdom and right action: Samkhya and Yoga, the two traditional Hindu philosophical systems discussed in chapter 2.

[3] Without concentration: literally, "without yoga."

[4] Spiritual: literally, "yoked to yoga."

[5] Saint: *tattvavid*, knower of truth.

5 □ The Renunciation of Action

Arjuna said:

1 My Lord! At one moment you praise renunciation of action; at another, right action. Tell me truly, I pray, which of these is the more conducive to my highest welfare?

Lord Shri Krishna replied:

2 Renunciation of action and the path of right action both lead to the highest; of the two, right action is the better.

3 He is a true ascetic[1] who never desires or dislikes, who is uninfluenced by the opposites and is easily freed from bondage.

4 Only the unenlightened speak of wisdom and right action[2] as separate; not the wise. If any man knows one, he enjoys the fruit of both.

5 The level which is reached by wisdom is attained through right action as well. He who perceives that the two are one knows the truth.

6 Without concentration,[3] O Mighty Man! renunciation is difficult. But the sage who is always meditating on the Divine, before long shall attain the Absolute.

7 He who is spiritual,[4] who is pure, who has overcome his senses and his personal self, who has realized his highest Self as the Self of all, such a one, even though he acts, is not bound by his acts.

8 Though the saint[5] sees, hears, touches, smells, eats, moves, sleeps, and breathes, yet he knows the Truth, and he knows that it is not he who acts.

6 "Dedicates his actions to the Spirit" suggests that all acts should be performed as offerings, for the sake of God. Some translators render the phrase as "casting all actions on Brahman" or "reposing all actions on Brahman." Ramanuja understands this as meaning we should realize that everything proceeds from Brahman, while we ourselves do nothing. Professor Edgerton agrees, reasoning: "Since Brahman or God is all, all acts must really be done by Him; and this despite the fact that elsewhere we are told often and clearly enough that all actions are done by Prakriti." Or so it appears to the limited mind. From the vantage point of awakened consciousness, God alone is, yet God does nothing, and everything that happens is ultimately an illusion. In order to arrive at this realization, however, we need to renounce our sense of being the doer, and one way to accomplish this is to carry out our duties with the attitude that it is the indwelling God who is getting them done through us.

7 Water lily: literally, a lotus leaf. The lotus (a plant of the water lily family) has its roots in the mud, but its blossom and leaves remain pure and unaffected as they float on top of the water. The lotus is thus a favorite symbol of the detachment of being "in the world but not of it."

8 The nine gates are the nine openings of the body: two eyes, two ears, two nostrils, mouth, genitals, and anus.

9 Wisdom: *vidya*, intuitive knowledge of the self as one with ultimate Reality; a synonym of *jnana* and *prajna*. Its opposite is *avidya* (often translated as "nescience," meaning "nonknowledge"), ignorance of the true nature of the self.

10 Infidel: *shvapaka* ("dog-cooker"), the lowest class of outcaste.

9 Though he talks, though he gives and receives, though he opens his eyes and shuts them, he still knows that his senses are merely disporting themselves among the objects of perception.

10 He who dedicates his actions to the Spirit,[6] without any personal attachment to them, he is no more tainted by sin than the water lily[7] is wetted by water.

11 The sage performs his action dispassionately, using his body, mind, and intellect, and even his senses, always as a means of purification.

12 Having abandoned the fruit of action, he wins eternal peace. Others, unacquainted with spirituality, led by desire and clinging to the benefit which they think will follow their actions, become entangled by them.

13 Mentally renouncing all actions, the self-controlled soul enjoys bliss in this body, the city of the nine gates,[8] neither doing anything himself nor causing anything to be done.

14 The Lord of this universe has not ordained activity, or any incentive thereto, or any relation between an act and its consequences. All this is the work of Nature.

15 The Lord does not accept responsibility for any man's sin or merit. Men are deluded because in them wisdom is submerged in ignorance.

16 Surely wisdom[9] is like the sun, revealing the supreme truth to those whose ignorance is dispelled by the wisdom of the Self.

17 Meditating on the Divine, having faith in the Divine, concentrating on the Divine, and losing themselves in the Divine, their sins dissolved in wisdom, they go whence there is no return.

18 Sages look equally upon all, whether it be a minister of learning and humility or an infidel,[10] or whether it be a cow, an elephant, or a dog.

19 Even in this world they conquer their earth-life whose minds, fixed on

11 Eternal Bliss: *brahma-nirvana*, "the *nirvana* of Brahman." See ch. 2, n. 32.

12 To "seek only the welfare of all" is, in Professor Edgerton's words, "perhaps the highest formulation of practical ethics that any religion has attained." (A similar ideal is expressed in 3.20, 3.25, and 12.4.) Work for the welfare of others is spiritually valuable only if it is selfless service, inspired by love for God. "If you render service in order to oblige a person and if you feel proud of doing it, you are not only doing spiritual harm to the recipient of your service but also to yourself. If, while serving, you take delight in it and develop pride in doing a good thing, you are getting attached to your act and thereby binding yourself" (Meher Baba).

13 Between the eyebrows: "When the eyes are half-closed in meditation, the eyeballs remain motionless, and their gaze converges toward a point between the brows" (Nikhilananda). That point is the *ajna chakra*, often called the "third eye," the center of inner vision and intuitive knowledge. "When the internal eye is opened, God—who is the object of search and longing—is actually sighted" (Meher Baba).

14 Inward and outward breathings: a reference to *pranayama* (see ch. 4, n. 16).

15 Eternal Peace: *shanti*, here meaning *brahma-nirvana*. This does not necessarily imply the death of the physical body (as "passing into Eternal Peace" might suggest in English). Ramanuja says that the person who knows the Lord as a Friend attains peace, meaning that he or she "wins happiness even while performing Karma Yoga." The practice of *karma yoga* is undertaken gladly because "All beings endeavor to please a friend."

the Supreme, remain always balanced, for the Supreme has neither blemish nor bias.

20 He who knows and lives in the Absolute remains unmoved and unperturbed; he is not elated by pleasure or depressed by pain.

21 He finds happiness in his own Self and enjoys eternal bliss, whose heart does not yearn for the contacts of earth, and whose Self is one with the Everlasting.

22 The joys that spring from external associations bring pain; they have their beginnings and their endings. The wise man does not rejoice in them.

23 He who, before he leaves his body, learns to surmount the promptings of desire and anger, is a saint, and is happy.

24 He who is happy within his Self, and has found its peace, and in whom the inner light shines, that sage attains Eternal Bliss[11] and becomes the Spirit itself.

25 Sages whose sins have been washed away, whose sense of separateness has vanished, who have subdued themselves and seek only the welfare of all,[12] come to the Eternal Spirit.

26 Saints who know their Selves, who control their minds and feel neither desire nor anger, find Eternal Bliss everywhere.

27 Excluding external objects, his gaze fixed between the eyebrows,[13] the inward and outward breathings[14] passing equally through his nostrils;

28 Governing sense, mind, and intellect, intent on liberation, free from desire, fear, and anger, the sage is forever free.

29 Knowing Me as Him who gladly receives all offerings of austerity and sacrifice, as the Mighty Ruler of all the worlds, and the Friend of all beings, he passes to Eternal Peace.[15]

@ *Dhyana*: meditation, the mind flowing in an unbroken stream toward an object of contemplation. *Dhyana* is the first stage of a process that eventually leads to *samadhi*, or concentration, in which the mind unites with its object.

1 Desire: *samkalpa*, will, purpose, "the imaginative faculty that plans for the future" (Besant). "Those thoughts causing the desires which impel one to action" (Shankara). "No one can be a karma yogi who makes plans and wishes for the fruit of action" (Swarupananda).

2 In verses 5–6 the word *atman* appears several times in such a way that it could mean either "self/Self," "soul," or "ego." According to Yogananda, the meaning is "Let man be uplifted, not degraded; let him transform his self (ego) into the Self (soul). The Self is the friend of the transformed self, but the enemy of the unregenerate self."

3 Wisdom: *jnana*; spiritual insight: *vijnana*. "*Jnana* is understanding through reason, and *vijnana* is that knowledge which sinks through reason into experience" (Gandhi). "A jnani is like one who knows beyond a doubt that a log of wood contains fire. But a vijnani is he who lights the log, cooks over the fire, and is nourished by the food" (Ramakrishna).

4 The saint (*yukta*, "disciplined") sees all beings and things of the world as "emanations from the one Divine Consciousness" (Yogananda). Some regard this yogic ideal of equality towards all beings as a kind of lofty indifference; however, the Gita also teaches the compassionate ideal of "working for the welfare of all beings" (12.4).

6 □ Meditation and Self-Control: Dhyana Yoga

Lord Shri Krishna said:

1 He who acts because it is his duty, not thinking of the consequences, is really spiritual and a true ascetic, and not he who merely observes rituals or who shuns all action.

2 O Arjuna! Renunciation is in fact what is called Right Action. No one can become spiritual who has not renounced all desire.[1]

3 For the sage who seeks the heights of spiritual meditation, practice is the only method, and when he has attained them, he must maintain himself there by continual self-control.

4 When a person renounces even the thought of initiating action, when he is not interested in sense objects or any results which may flow from his acts, then in truth he understands spirituality.

5 Let him seek liberation by the help of his highest Self, and let him never disgrace his own Self. For that Self is his only friend; yet it may also be his enemy.

6 To him who has conquered his lower nature by its help, the Self is a friend, but to him who has not done so, it is an enemy.[2]

7 The Self of him who is self-controlled and has attained peace is equally unmoved by heat or cold, pleasure or pain, honor or dishonor.

8 He who desires nothing but wisdom and spiritual insight,[3] who has conquered his senses and who looks with the same eye upon a lump of earth, a stone, or fine gold, is the real saint.[4]

5 This verse refers to the ideal conditions for meditation. "Unceasingly" means daily, during meditation practice; "seclusion" means a quiet, undisturbed place; "absolutely alone" means meditating by oneself (Ramanuja). One should not expect to have any particular experience, and should have no sense of possessing anything other than the self. "Meditation is a process which takes the mind from the consciousness of possessions to the consciousness of Being" (Maharishi).

6 The sacred *kusha* grass, deer (or tiger) skin, and cloth traditionally used by yogis provide insulation from damp and "earth currents" (Yogananda). The forest-dwelling yogis of India used the skins of animals that had died naturally. Yogananda suggests using a wool blanket and a silk cloth as substitutes.

7 Mind concentrated: *ekagra,* one-pointed. One-pointedness is a primary technique of yoga. By focusing attention on a single object of meditation, one withdraws attention from the activity of the life force in the senses, a self-purifying process.

8 Yogananda identifies the focus as the point between the eyebrows (see ch. 5, n. 13). Sri Aurobindo's translation reads, "he shall keep his gaze fixed on the joining point of the nostrils" (where the breath goes in and out). Maharishi translates the phrase "having directed his gaze to the front of his nose," and notes, "Shankara says that if fixing the gaze on the tip of the nose were meant here, the mind would be left with the nose but without God." The actual meaning, according to Shankara, is "fixing of the eyesight within." The eyes are not really looking at anything, but the line of sight converges near the tip of the nose. The important thing is the focusing of the internal attention and the centering of the mind in the Self.

9 Vow of celibacy: *brahmacharya,* the way of life of a religious student, which includes sexual abstinence. "It is not...the act of taking a vow that is emphasized here; rather, it is the secure and safeguarded upward flow of one's energies on the road to the divine quest" (Maharishi).

9 He looks impartially on all—lover, friend, or foe; indifferent or hostile; alien or relative; virtuous or sinful.

10 Let the student of spirituality try unceasingly to concentrate his mind; let him live in seclusion, absolutely alone, with mind and personality controlled, free from desire, and without possessions.[5]

11 Having chosen a holy place, let him sit in a firm posture on a seat neither too high nor too low, and covered with a grass mat, a deer skin, and a cloth.[6]

12 Seated thus, his mind concentrated,[7] its functions controlled, and his senses governed, let him practice meditation for the purification of his lower nature.

13 Let him hold body, head, and neck erect, motionless, and steady; let him look fixedly at the tip of his nose,[8] turning neither to the right nor to the left.

14 With peace in his heart and no fear, observing the vow of celibacy,[9] with mind controlled and fixed on Me, let the student lose himself in contemplation of Me.

15 Thus keeping his mind always in communion with me, and with his thoughts subdued, he shall attain that Peace which is Mine and which will lead him to liberation at last.

16 Meditation is not for one who eats too much, nor for one who eats not at all: nor for one who is overmuch addicted to sleep, nor for one who is always awake.

17 But for one who regulates food and recreation, who is balanced in action, in sleep and in waking, it shall dispel all unhappiness.

18 When the mind, completely controlled, is centered in the Self and free from all earthly desires, then is a person truly spiritual.

19 The wise man who has conquered his mind and is absorbed in the Self is

[10] Pure Intellect: *buddhi*.

[11] Heart: *chetas*, a synonym for *chitta* (see ch. 4, n. 11). In Indian philosophy, "heart" is considered an aspect of mind, concerned with intuitive understanding and valuation.

[12] Mind: *manas*. Because of its wandering nature, *manas* is often called the "monkey mind."

[13] "Since one's own Self or Soul is really identical with the Self or Soul of all other creatures, therefore one who injures others injures himself.... Thus one of the most striking and emphatic of the ethical doctrines of the Gita is substantially that of the Golden Rule" (Edgerton). "'To love your neighbor as yourself' is inherent in the Vedic formula of unity with the absolute self, 'That art thou' *(tat tvam asi)*. Because one loves oneself, one is bound to love one's neighbor, who is not different from oneself" *(Encyclopedia of Religion)*. Similar verses are 4.35 and 5.7.

as a lamp which does not flicker, since it stands sheltered from every wind.

20 There, where the whole nature is seen in the light of the Self, where the person abides within his Self and is satisfied, there, its functions restrained by its union with the Divine, the mind finds rest.

21 When he enjoys the bliss which passes sense, and which only the Pure Intellect[10] can grasp, when he comes to rest within his own highest Self, never again will he stray from reality.

22 Finding That, he will realize that there is no possession so precious. And when once established there, no calamity can disturb him.

23 This inner severance from the affliction of misery is spirituality. It should be practiced with determination, and with a heart[11] which refuses to be depressed.

24 Renouncing every desire which imagination can conceive, controlling the senses at every point by the power of mind;

25 Little by little, by the help of his reason controlled by fortitude, let him attain peace; and, fixing his mind on the Self, let him not think of any other thing.

26 When the volatile and wavering mind would wander,[12] let him restrain it, and bring it again to its allegiance to the Self.

27 Supreme bliss is the lot of the sage whose mind attains Peace, whose passions subside, who is without sin, and who becomes one with the Absolute.

28 Thus, free from sin, abiding always in the Eternal, the saint enjoys without effort the bliss which flows from realization of the Infinite.

29 He who experiences the unity of life sees his own Self in all beings and all beings in his own Self, and looks on everything with an impartial eye;[13]

14 Practice *(abhyasa)* and renunciation *(vairagya)* are two important aspects of spiritual life. "The word *renunciation* sounds grim; but in fact it means renouncing the smaller for the greater, sweetened milk for ice cream" (Prabhavananda). *Vairagya* implies equanimity and dispassion, in which attachment to lower values naturally falls away as one is drawn more powerfully to higher truths. "Unless practice is accompanied by an attitude of dispassion, one runs the risk of inflating rather than transcending the ego," while dispassion without practice "may lead to confusion and possibly delusion instead of liberation" (Feuerstein).

@ "When a man of the world praised an Indian ascetic for his powers of renunciation, the yogi responded: 'Your renunciation is far greater than mine, for I have renounced the finite for the Infinite, whereas you are renouncing the Infinite for the finite.'" —Huston Smith

30 He who sees Me in everything and everything in Me, him shall I never forsake, nor shall he lose Me.

31 The sage who realizes the unity of life and who worships Me in all beings, lives in Me, whatever may be his lot.

32 O Arjuna! He is the perfect saint who, taught by the likeness within himself, sees the same Self everywhere, whether the outer form be pleasurable or painful.

Arjuna said:

33 I do not see how I can attain this state of equanimity which you have revealed, owing to the restlessness of my mind.

34 My Lord! Verily, the mind is fickle and turbulent, obstinate and strong, yea extremely difficult as the wind to control.

Lord Shri Krishna replied:

35 Doubtless, O Mighty One! the mind is fickle and exceedingly difficult to restrain, but, O son of Kunti! with practice and renunciation[14] it can be done.

36 It is not possible to attain Self-Realization if a man does not know how to control himself; but for him who, striving by proper means, learns such control, it is possible.

Arjuna asked:

37 He who fails to control himself, whose mind falls from spiritual contemplation, who attains not perfection but retains his faith, what of him, my Lord?

38 Having failed in both, my Lord! is he without hope, like a riven cloud having no support, lost on the spiritual road?

39 My Lord! You are worthy to solve this doubt once for all; besides Yourself, there is no one competent to do so.

15 Earnestly strives: Effort *(prayatna)* is necessary on the spiritual path, although ultimate success depends on the grace of God or the Master. Divine grace is constantly pouring forth; effort helps one to receive it. Meher Baba likens grace to "rain which falls on all lands, barren and fertile, but fructifies only in the lands that have been rendered fertile through toil."

Two schools of thought differ over the question of effort versus grace. Those who exert effort are likened to a baby monkey, who holds on to its mother as she swings through the trees, while those who rely solely on grace are like the baby cat, whose mother carries it by the scruff of the neck. In both cases, however, it is the mother (God) who carries the baby (aspirant) where it needs to go.

16 "Wise man" here translates *yogi*, one who practices disciplined activity, defined as "doing unselfishly whatever action seems to be required in any given circumstances" (Edgerton). The yogi is contrasted here with the "man of action," meaning one who performs religious rituals.

Lord Shri Krishna replied:

40 My beloved child! There is no destruction for him, either in this world or in the next. No evil fate awaits him who treads the path of righteousness.

41 Having reached the worlds where the righteous dwell, and having remained there for many years, he who has slipped away from the path of spirituality will be born again in the family of the pure, benevolent, and prosperous.

42 Or he may be born in the family of the wise sages; though a birth like this is, indeed, very difficult to obtain.

43 Then the experience acquired in his former life will revive, and with its help he will strive for perfection more eagerly than before.

44 Unconsciously he will return to the practices of his old life; so that he who tries to realize spiritual consciousness is certainly superior to one who only talks of it.

45 Then, after many lives, the student of spirituality who earnestly strives,[15] and whose sins are absolved, attains perfection and reaches the Supreme.

46 The wise man[16] is superior to the ascetic and to the scholar and to the man of action; therefore be a wise man, O Arjuna!

47 I look upon him as the best of mystics who, full of faith, worships Me and abides in Me.

1 "The vast masses of mankind are content with material things; but there are some who are awake and want to get back, who have had enough of this playing here. These struggle consciously, while the rest do it unconsciously" (Vivekananda). "We should look upon ourselves as those exceptional persons among thousands" (Gandhi).

2 Ether: *akasha*, all-pervasive space, the finest of the five elements (see ch. 13, n. 2).

3 Mind, intellect, and personality: *manas, buddhi,* and *ahamkara.*

4 Manifested Nature: Prakriti. See ch. 2, n. 8.

5 "Contemplating matter, the soul becomes entangled in the world; contemplating the Spirit, it attains liberation. Hence the Spirit-form of the Lord is superior to His matter-form" (Nikhilananda).

6 Worlds created and dissolved: see ch. 8, n. 7.

7 OM: This sacred syllable, expressive of the highest cosmic consciousness, may be called a mantra (sacred utterance), a name of God, or a primordial creative vibration that pervades the universe. It is described as an approximation of the "sound of the soundless Absolute." The word appears at the beginning of written works and may be uttered at the beginning and end of a prayer or recitation from the scriptures. The kinship of OM with the Hebrew *amen* and Arabic *amin* ("so be it") is pointed out by Meher Baba, who adds, "Coming from a man, 'So be it' is a blessing or a wish; but coming from God it is creation." Yogananda also links OM to the Tibetan mantra HUM.

OM is sometimes spelled AUM, because it is made up of three sounds

7 □ Knowledge and Experience

Lord Shri Krishna said:

1 Listen, O Arjuna! And I will tell you how you shall know Me in My full perfection, practicing meditation with your mind devoted to Me, and having Me for your refuge.

2 I will reveal this knowledge unto you, and how it may be realized; which, once accomplished, there remains nothing else worth having in this life.

3 Among thousands of people, scarcely one strives for perfection,[1] and even among those who gain occult powers, perchance but one knows Me in truth.

4 Earth, water, fire, air, ether,[2] mind, intellect, and personality[3]—this is the eightfold division of My Manifested Nature.[4]

5 This is My inferior Nature; but distinct from this, O Valiant One! know that My Superior Nature is the very Life which sustains the universe.[5]

6 It is the womb of all being; for I am He by whom the worlds were created and shall be dissolved.[6]

7 O Arjuna! There is nothing higher than Me; all is strung upon Me as rows of pearls upon a thread.

8 O Arjuna! I am the Fluidity in water, the Light in the sun and in the moon. I am the mystic syllable OM[7] in the Vedic scriptures, the Sound in ether, the Virility in man.

9 I am the Fragrance of earth, the Brilliance of fire. I am the Life Force in all beings, and I am the Austerity of the ascetics.

(the letter o consisting of the sounds *a* and *u*), which, respectively, are compared to three states of consciousness: waking (equated with the gross realm of manifestation), dreaming (subtle), and sleeping (causal). The syllable as a whole indicates a fourth state (*turiya,* "fourth")—the state of the transcendental Self.

8 Attachment: *raga.* Desire: *kama.*

9 Although desire has been declared to be the enemy (3.37), the desire for truth or righteousness *(dharma)* is the one desire that eventually ends all desire. "The only Real Desire is to see God, and the only Real Longing is to become one with God. This Real Desire and Longing frees one from the bondage of birth and death. Other desires and longings bind one with ignorance" (Meher Baba).

10 "It is like a mirage in the desert. From the standpoint of the onlooker, the illusory water exists in the desert; but the desert does not depend upon or exist in the mirage. Likewise the universe, apparently superimposed on the Lord, exists in the Lord, but the Lord is not in the universe" (Nikhilananda).

11 Divine Illusion: Maya, the creative power that makes the illusory world of duality appear real; "the deluding cosmic hypnosis" (Yogananda). In the Gita, Maya is identified with Nature (Prakriti) and the three Qualities. Although it creates the false illusion of the finite world, in itself it is "divine in its power and therefore difficult to overcome" (Ramanuja). An aspect of the Goddess, Maya is inscrutable. Jnanadeva says: "Maya both is and is not. She is as impossible to describe as the child of a barren woman.... Only through her does the splendor of the Supreme become manifest."

"Even though the Lord manifests through maya, the tangible relative universe, and appears to be its cause and support, yet He is always One and without a second, transcendental, incorporeal, and unattached. This is His eternal mystery" (Nikhilananda). This paradox of the ultimate Reality was often alluded to by Sri Ramana Maharshi by quoting a well-known saying attributed to Shankara: "The world is illusory; Brahman alone is real; Brahman is the world."

10 Know, O Arjuna! that I am the eternal Seed of being; I am the Intelligence of the intelligent, the Splendor of the resplendent.

11 I am the Strength of the strong, of them who are free from attachment and desire;[8] and, O Arjuna! I am the Desire for righteousness.[9]

12 Whatever be the nature of their life, whether it be Pure or Passionate or Ignorant, they all are derived from Me. They are in Me, but I am not in them.[10]

13 The inhabitants of this world, misled by those natures which the Qualities have engendered, know not that I am higher than them all, and that I do not change.

14 Verily, this Divine Illusion[11] of Phenomena manifesting itself in the Qualities is difficult to surmount. Only they who devote themselves to Me and to Me alone can accomplish it.

15 The sinner, the ignorant, the vile, deprived of spiritual perception by the glamour of Illusion, and he who pursues a godless life—none of them shall find Me.

16 O Arjuna! The righteous who worship Me are grouped by stages: first they who suffer, next they who desire knowledge, then they who thirst after truth, and lastly they who attain wisdom.

17 Of all these, he who has gained wisdom, who meditates on Me without ceasing, devoting himself only to Me, he is the best; for by the wise man I am exceedingly beloved, and the wise man, too, is beloved by Me.

18 Noble-minded are they all, but the wise man I hold as my own Self; for he, remaining always at peace with Me, makes Me his final goal.

19 After many lives, at last the wise man realizes Me as I am. A man so enlightened that he sees God everywhere is very difficult to find.

20 They in whom wisdom is obscured by one desire or the other worship the lesser Powers, practicing many rites, which vary according to their temperaments.

12 In India it is customary to worship the form *(murti)* of a deity—for example, to place food, fruits, and flowers before an image of Krishna, or to pray or meditate before it. Even just viewing a divine form (an act known as *darshana,* "sight, vision")—whether it is a statue, a painting, or the living presence of a spiritually perfect person—"is an act of worship, and through the eyes one gains the blessing of the divine" (Eck). However, although meditation on the form of a deity or a perfect one helps the aspirant to absorb divine qualities into his or her own being, it is unwise to overemphasize the physical form. The body of Krishna was merely a coat that he put on to make himself visible to the world. One must strive to see the Avatar as he really is, in his all-pervading infinite being—which in reality is our own Self. "He who worships God merely as a finite form will not attain the transcendental divine union with His infinite nature" (Yogananda).

@ "Age after age the infinite God wills through His infinite mercy to come among mankind by descending to the human level in a human form. His physical presence among mankind is not understood and He is looked upon as an ordinary man of the world. When He asserts His divinity by proclaiming Himself the Avatar of the age, He is worshipped by some who accept Him as God, and glorified by a few who know him as God on earth. It happens invariably, though, that the rest of humanity condemns Him while He is physically among them."

—Meher Baba

13 The life of the world: Adhibhuta, that which underlies all the elements.

14 The universal sacrifice: Adhiyajna, the lord of sacrifice.

15 Pure Divinity: Adhidaiva, that which underlies all the gods.

21 But whatever the form of worship, if the devotee have faith, then upon his faith in that worship do I set My own seal.

22 If he worships one form alone with real faith, then shall his desires be fulfilled through that only; for thus have I ordained.

23 The fruit that comes to men of limited insight is, after all, finite. They who worship the Lower Powers attain them; but those who worship Me come unto Me alone.

24 The ignorant think of Me, who am the Unmanifested Spirit, as if I were really in human form. They do not understand that My Supreme Nature is changeless and most excellent.¹²

25 I am not visible to all, for I am enveloped by the Illusion of Phenomena. This deluded world does not know Me as the Unborn and the Imperishable.

26 I know, O Arjuna! all beings in the past, the present, and the future; but they do not know Me.

27 O brave Arjuna! Man lives in a fairy world, deceived by the glamour of opposite sensations, infatuated by desire and aversion.

28 But those who act righteously, in whom sin has been destroyed, who are free from the infatuation of the conflicting emotions, they worship Me with firm resolution.

29 Those who make Me their refuge, who strive for liberation from decay and death, they realize the Supreme Spirit, which is their own real Self, and in which all action finds its consummation.

30 Those who see Me in the life of the world, ¹³ in the universal sacrifice,¹⁴ and as pure Divinity,¹⁵ keeping their minds steady, they live in Me, even in the crucial hour of death.

1 Supreme Spirit: Brahman.

2 Spiritual Nature: Adhyatma, one's essential self.

3 Law: a translation of *karman* (action), which has several meanings. It is the law of karma by which our own actions cause us to be born in particular conditions. It can mean all cosmic or divine activities as well as the spiritual and worldly actions of human beings. *Karman* also means the sacrificial act of making ritual offerings to the gods.

4 A classic example from the Puranas (ancient texts of mythology and divine legend) is King Bharata, whose dying thought was of his pet deer, and so he was reborn as a deer. The thought at death will typically be the habitual thought of one's lifetime; therefore one must practice remembering God and repeating one's favorite divine name as often as possible.

8 □ The Supreme Spirit

Arjuna asked:

1 O Lord of Lords! What is that which is called the Supreme Spirit,[1] what is man's Spiritual Nature,[2] and what is the Law?[3] What is Matter and what is Divinity?

2 Who is it who rules the spirit of sacrifice in man; and at the time of death how may those who have learned self-control come to the knowledge of You?

The Lord Shri Krishna replied:

3 The Supreme Spirit is the Highest Imperishable Self, and Its Nature is spiritual consciousness. The worlds have been created and are supported by an emanation from the Spirit which is called the Law.

4 Matter consists of the forms that perish; Divinity is the Supreme Self; and He who inspires the spirit of sacrifice in man, O noblest of your race! is I myself, Who now stand in human form before you.

5 Whosoever at the time of death thinks only of Me, and thinking thus leaves the body and goes forth, assuredly he will know Me.

6 On whatever sphere of being the mind of a man may be intent at the time of death, thither will he go.[4]

7 Therefore meditate always on Me, and fight; if your mind and your reason be fixed on Me, to Me shall you surely come.

8 He whose mind does not wander, and who is engaged in constant meditation, attains the Supreme Spirit.

5 Passion: *raga*, attachment to pleasure.

6 Vow of continence: *brahmacharya*. See ch. 6, n. 9.

7 Cycles: *mahayugas*, or "great ages." A *mahayuga* is made up of four *yugas*, or ages (see ch. 4. n. 6), and is said to last 4,320,000 years. One thousand such cycles equal one *kalpa*. At the end of the cosmic "day of Brahma," the dissolution *(pralaya)* of the universe occurs, in which the phenomenal world is withdrawn from manifest existence. During the night of Brahma, "only the subtle dimensions of the cosmos, inhabited by the deities and sages, exist. When Brahma awakens from his sleep, the world is created anew" (Feuerstein). After a cycle of cycles the entire universe—including the god of creation itself, Brahma—is absorbed back into the absolute Brahman in a great dissolution *(mahapralaya)*.

9 Whoso meditates on the Omniscient, the Ancient, more minute than the atom, yet the Ruler and Upholder of all, Unimaginable, Brilliant like the Sun, beyond the reach of darkness;

10 He who leaves the body with mind unmoved and filled with devotion, by the power of his meditation gathering between his eyebrows his whole vital energy, attains the Supreme.

11 Now I will speak briefly of the imperishable goal, proclaimed by those versed in the scriptures, which the mystic attains when free from passion,[5] and for which he is content to undergo the vow of continence.[6]

12 Closing the gates of the body, drawing the forces of his mind into the heart, and by the power of meditation concentrating his vital energy in the brain;

13 Repeating OM, the Symbol of Eternity, holding Me always in remembrance, he who thus leaves his body and goes forth reaches the Spirit Supreme.

14 To him who thinks constantly of Me and of nothing else, to such an ever-faithful devotee, O Arjuna! am I ever accessible.

15 Coming thus unto Me, these great souls go no more to the misery and death of earthly life, for they have gained perfection.

16 The worlds, with the whole realm of creation, come and go; but, O Arjuna! whoso comes to Me, for him there is no rebirth.

17 Those who understand the cosmic day and cosmic night know that one day of creation is a thousand cycles, and that the night is of equal length.[7]

18 At the dawning of that day all objects in manifestation stream forth from the Unmanifest, and when evening falls they are dissolved into It again.

19 The same multitude of beings, which have lived on earth so often, all are dissolved as the night of the universe approaches, to issue forth anew

8 The Eternal Unmanifest is an imperishable state distinct from the Unmanifest Spirit of Creation, *avyakata* (see below, n. 9, and ch. 13, n. 2).

9 The Unmanifest Spirit of Creation *(avyakata)* is likened by Yogananda to a temporary resting place for souls that have not achieved enlightenment at the time of cosmic dissolution. They continue their journey when a new cycle of creation issues forth.

10 Verses 23–26: "Different courses after death have been pointed out by the Hindu scriptures in order to warn people against neglecting Self-knowledge and to exhort them to realize Brahman, which alone is the source of peace and happiness. According to the Hindu scriptures, all living beings, without any exception whatsoever, will attain Self-knowledge and liberation" (Nikhilananda).

"Mystics who are advanced in yoga practice can arrange the time and place to leave the body. Others have no control—if by accident they leave at an auspicious moment, then they will not return to the cycle of birth and death, but if not, then there is every possibility that they will have to return. However, for the pure devotee in Krishna consciousness, there is no fear of returning, whether he leaves the body at an auspicious or inauspicious moment, by accident or arrangement" (Bhaktivedanta).

11 Six months before the Northern summer solstice: The six months of the sun's northward course according to Vedic astrology are from the middle of January to the middle of July. The day on which the sun begins its journey to the Northern Hemisphere (when the sun enters the sign of Capricorn) is a day of celebration known as Makar Sankranti, observed by Hindus every January 14.

12 Therefore meditate perpetually; alternatively, "at all times be in Yoga" (Aurobindo).

when morning breaks. Thus is it ordained.

20 In truth, therefore, there is the Eternal Unmanifest,[8] which is beyond and above the Unmanifest Spirit of Creation,[9] which is never destroyed when all these beings perish.

21 The wise say that the Unmanifest and Indestructible is the highest goal of all; when once that is reached, there is no return. That is My Blessed Home.

22 O Arjuna! That Highest God, in whom all beings abide, and who pervades the entire universe, is reached only by whole-hearted devotion.

23 Now I will tell you, O Arjuna! of the times at which, if the mystics go forth, they do not return, and at which they go forth only to return.[10]

24 If, knowing the Supreme Spirit, the sage goes forth with fire and light, in the daytime, in the fortnight of the waxing moon, and in the six months before the Northern summer solstice,[11] he will attain the Supreme.

25 But if he departs in gloom, at night, during the fortnight of the waning moon and in the six months before the Southern solstice, then he reaches but lunar light, and he will be born again.

26 These bright and dark paths out of the world have always existed. Whoso takes the former returns not; he who chooses the latter returns.

27 O Arjuna! The saint knowing these paths is not confused. Therefore meditate perpetually.[12]

28 The sage who knows this passes beyond all merit that comes from the study of the scriptures, from sacrifice, from austerities and charity, and reaches the Supreme Primeval Abode.

1 Secret: *guhya*. Mystical teachings are secret because they are hidden from the ordinary person—not because anyone is deliberately hiding them or making them unavailable, but because the ordinary person's understanding is so deluded that he or she simply does not recognize, believe, or value the "secret" of liberation.

2 Faith: *shraddha*. See Sri Easwaran's definition on page 130.

3 Perishable world: *samsara*, the domain of birth, death, and rebirth; the transient existence to which we are bound by karma in a seemingly endless cycle, until we attain liberation.

4 "The Lord is always neutral, although He has His hand in every sphere of activity" (Bhaktivedanta). "He is interested in everything but not concerned about anything. The slightest mishap may command His sympathy; the greatest tragedy will not upset Him" (Meher Baba).

9 □ The Sovereign Secret

Lord Shri Krishna said:

1 I will now reveal to you, since you doubt not, that profound mysticism which, when followed by experience, shall liberate you from sin.

2 This is the Premier Science, the Sovereign Secret,[1] the Purest and Best; intuitional, righteous; and to him who practices it, pleasant beyond measure.

3 They who have no faith[2] in this teaching cannot find Me, but remain lost in the purlieus of this perishable world.[3]

4 The whole world is pervaded by Me, yet my form is not seen. All living things have their being in Me, yet I am not limited by them.

5 Nevertheless, they do not consciously abide in Me. Such is My Divine Sovereignty that though I, the Supreme Self, am the cause and upholder of all, yet I remain outside.

6 As the mighty wind, though moving everywhere, has no resting place but space, so have all these beings no home but Me.

7 All beings, O Arjuna! return at the close of every cosmic cycle into the realm of Nature, which is a part of Me, and at the beginning of the next I send them forth again.

8 With the help of Nature, again and again I pour forth the whole multitude of beings, whether they will or no, for they are ruled by My will.

9 But these acts of Mine do not bind Me. I remain outside and unattached.[4]

5 The "Father," "Mother," and "Grandfather" refer to different aspects of the Divine. The Grandfather is *paratpar-parabrahman*, the original, unmanifest "vacuum" state of God, so utterly transcendent that nothing can be said about it except "God is." The Father is *saguna-brahman*, Brahman with qualities; this is the personal deity worshiped as the One God under different names in different religions. The Mother is *mula-prakriti*, primordial Nature, through which the Supreme becomes manifest. Krishna, as the Avatar, is all of these in one.

"Kabir [a great poet-saint] used to say, 'The formless Absolute is my Father, and God with form is my Mother.' God reveals Himself in the form which His devotee loves most. His love for the devotee knows no bounds" (Ramakrishna).

6 *Soma* (literally "juice") is regarded as the receptacle of *amrita* ("non-death"), nectar of immortality. In Vedic sacrificial rituals, *soma* was made into an intoxicating drink, offered to the gods, and then drunk by the priests; scholars do not agree on what plant it came from, though some believe it was a hallucinogenic mushroom. *Soma* or *amrita* also refers to a subtle rejuvenating substance that flows from a center (chakra) in the head. "The nectar's flow increases when the 'serpent power' [*kundalini*, divine cosmic energy] has ascended from the base center to the psychoenergetic center at the throat" (Feuerstein).

10 Under My guidance, Nature produces all things movable and immovable. Thus it is, O Arjuna! that this universe revolves.

11 Fools disregard Me, seeing Me clad in human form. They know not that in My higher nature I am the Lord God of all.

12 Their hopes are vain, their actions worthless, their knowledge futile; they are without sense, deceitful, barbarous, and godless.

13 But the Great Souls, O Arjuna! filled with my Divine Spirit, they worship Me, they fix their minds on Me and on Me alone, for they know that I am the imperishable Source of being.

14 Always extolling Me, strenuous, firm in their vows, prostrating themselves before Me, they worship Me continually with concentrated devotion.

15 Others worship Me with full consciousness, as the One, the Manifold, the Omnipresent, the Universal.

16 I am the Oblation, the Sacrifice, and the Worship; I am the Fuel and the Chant, I am the Butter offered to the fire, I am the Fire itself; and I am the Act of offering.

17 I am the Father of the universe and its Mother; I am its Nourisher and its Grandfather;[5] I am the Knowable and the Pure; I am OM; and I am the Sacred Scriptures.

18 I am the Goal, the Sustainer, the Lord, the Witness, the Home, the Shelter, the Lover, and the Origin; I am Life and Death; I am the Fountain and the Seed Imperishable.

19 I am the Heat of the Sun. I release and hold back the Rains. I am Death and Immortality; I am Being and Not-Being.

20 Those who are versed in the scriptures, who drink the mystic Soma juice[6] and are purified from sin, but who, while worshiping Me with sacrifices, pray that I will lead them to heaven—they reach the holy world

7 Controller of the Powers of Nature: Indra, lord of the gods.

8 I will take upon Myself the fulfillment of his aspiration: Other translators read the meaning as "I will carry to him everything he needs." Prabhavananda recounts the following story. A scholar who was writing a commentary on the Gita was puzzled by this verse: how could Lord Krishna literally *carry* to his devotee everything he needs? So he scratched out the phrase *vahamyaham* (I carry) and substituted *dadmyaham* (I supply). Now, the scholar worked as a priest in a distant village and earned only enough for the daily needs of his family. It happened that on the day he scratched out that phrase from the Gita, when he went to do his priestly duty, a violent storm prevented him from returning home. He worried all night that his wife and children would go hungry until his return. On arriving home the next day, the scholar apologized and explained about the storm. But his wife said, "Why, you sent a boy who carried a basket of food for us, and we had a delightful meal. But how could you be so cruel to that young boy? He said you scratched his forehead three times, and there were traces of blood." Then suddenly the priest realized that it was the Lord himself who had carried to them what they needed. So in the edition of the Gita that he was commenting on, he repeated the phrase *vahamyaham* three times: "I carry, I carry, I carry."

9 "The right method is to have no intermediary between oneself and God. 'But,' Shri Krishna says, 'those who seek Me through the gatekeepers that stand between, they too worship Me, for they worship these in order to reach Me'" (Gandhi).

10 "The practical approach to this verse is to look upon everything that we do, no matter how seemingly insignificant, as a gift to the Lord" (Easwaran).

"Worship also includes mental worship. You do not need to gather flowers and all the other paraphernalia for worship. You can mentally offer flowers and all the items you can think of to the Lord" (Prabhavananda).

where lives the Controller of the Powers of Nature,[7] and they enjoy the feasts of Paradise.

21 Yet although they enjoy the spacious glories of Paradise, nevertheless, when their merit is exhausted, they are born again into this world of mortals. They have followed the letter of the scriptures, yet because they have sought but to fulfill their own desires, they must depart and return again and again.

22 But if a man will meditate on Me and Me alone, and will worship Me always and everywhere, I will take upon Myself the fulfillment of his aspiration, and I will safeguard whatsoever he shall attain.[8]

23 Even those who worship the lesser Powers, if they do so with faith, they thereby worship Me, though not in the right way.[9]

24 I am the willing recipient of sacrifice, and I am its true Lord. But these do not know Me in truth, and so they sink back.

25 The votaries of the lesser Powers go to them; the devotees of spirits go to them; they who worship the Powers of Darkness, to such Powers shall they go; and so, too, those who worship Me shall come unto Me.

26 Whatever someone offers to Me, whether it be a leaf, or a flower, or fruit, or water, I accept it, for it is offered with devotion and purity of mind.[10]

27 Whatever you do, whatever you eat, whatever you sacrifice and give, whatever austerities you practice, do all as an offering to Me.

28 So shall your action be attended by no result, either good or bad; but through the spirit of renunciation you shall come to Me and be free.

29 I am the same to all beings. I favor none, and I hate none. But those who worship Me devotedly, they live in Me, and I in them.

30 Even the most sinful, if he worship Me with his whole heart, shall be considered righteous, for he is treading the right path.

11 Everyone has an equal opportunity to reach the goal of life, because in reality all beings are already one with God. "Children of sinful parents" (a reference to outcastes, believed to have taken low births because of bad karma), merchants (vaishyas), laborers (shudras), and women were all traditionally barred from studying the Vedas. But low social status, lack of education, failure to adhere to ritual and dogma, and sinfulness are not obstacles to spiritual progress for those who have one-pointed devotion.

Even people who hate or fear the Lord can reach the same destination as those who love him, if their hatred or fear causes them to remember him constantly and exclusively. Examples such as King Shishupala and the demonic Kamsa in the *Mahabharata* are cited to show that enemies of Krishna have attained liberation. Such one-pointed hatred that excludes all worldly attachment is rare, however, and in 16.19 Krishna indicates that hatred is not the correct path.

12 The first words of this much-quoted verse are sometimes translated, "Be Me-minded" *(manmana)*. Constant remembrance of the Lord should flow like an unbroken stream of oil poured from one vessel to another (Ramanuja). "When the mind in an unbroken stream thinks of the Lord, we have what is called para-bhakti, or supreme love" *(Devi-Bhagavata)*.

13 Surrender to Me: "The three most important things on the path of God-realization are love, obedience, and surrender.... The one who loves, desires to do the will of the beloved and seeks union with the beloved. Obedience performs the will of the beloved and seeks the pleasure of the beloved. Surrender resigns to the will of the beloved and seeks nothing" (Meher Baba).

31 He shall attain spirituality ere long, and Eternal Peace shall be his. O
Arjuna! Believe Me, My devotee is never lost.

32 For even the children of sinful parents, and those miscalled the weaker
sex, and merchants, and laborers, if only they will make Me their refuge,
they shall attain the Highest.[11]

33 What need then to mention the holy ministers of God, the devotees,
and the saintly rulers? You, therefore, born in this changing and miserable world, should worship Me too.

34 Fix your mind on Me,[12] devote yourself to Me, sacrifice for Me, surrender to Me,[13] make Me the object of your aspirations, and too shall
assuredly become one with Me, Who am your own Self.

1 The professors of divinity nor the great ascetics: God cannot be understood by the mind, nor can he be realized by practicing austerities. He can only be won by love.

2 Harmlessness *(ahimsa)* is one of the most important principles of Hinduism. When asked for his definition of *ahimsa*, Gandhi replied: "the avoidance of harm to any living creature in thought or deed." People often find it puzzling that Krishna urges Arjuna to fight, while at the same time extolling nonviolence in several passages. They wonder how a spiritual teaching can condone killing. See ch. 16, n. 3, for further comments on nonviolence.

3 The seven Great Seers *(maharishis):* archetypal teachers of spiritual wisdom to humanity, to whom the Vedas were revealed.

4 The Ancient Four: primordial figures, called Manus, who, like Adam, were progenitors of the human race as well as the earliest lawgivers. "I take this to imply that the human race is founded by a Manu at the beginning of each of the four world-ages *(yugas)*" (Edgerton). Purohit Swami identifies the four as Sanaka, Sanandana, Sanatana, and Sanatkumara—all sons of Brahma the Creator. See also ch. 4, n. 1.

5 The original Sanskrit text for verse 9 includes "speaking of Me constantly." "There comes a time in the growth of a spiritual aspirant when it becomes impossible for him to talk of anything but God, and if he hears of any worldly topics, he runs away" (Prabhavananda).

10 □ The Divine Manifestations

Lord Shri Krishna said:

1 Now, O Prince! Listen to My supreme advice, which I give you for the sake of your welfare, for you are My beloved.

2 Neither the professors of divinity nor the great ascetics[1] know my origin, for I am the source of them all.

3 He who knows Me as the unborn, without beginning, the Lord of the universe, he, stripped of his delusions, becomes free from all conceivable sin.

4 Intelligence, wisdom, non-illusion, forgiveness, truth, self-control, calmness, pleasure, pain, birth, death, fear and fearlessness;

5 Harmlessness,[2] equanimity, contentment, austerity, beneficence, fame and failure, all these, the characteristics of beings, spring from Me only.

6 The seven Great Seers,[3] the Progenitors of mankind, the Ancient Four,[4] and the Lawgivers were born of My will and came forth direct from Me. The race of humankind has sprung from them.

7 He who rightly understands My manifested glory and My Creative Power, beyond doubt attains perfect Peace.

8 I am the source of all; from Me everything flows. Therefore the wise worship Me with unchanging devotion.

9 With minds concentrated on Me,[5] with lives absorbed in Me, and enlightening each other, they ever feel content and happy.

10 To those who are always devout and who worship Me with love, I give

6 Supreme Spirit: *parabrahman*. *Para* means "supreme." Lord Krishna is one with Brahman, the ultimate nondual Reality, and with Atman, which means both the universal Self and the individual self or soul.

7 Eternal Divine Self: Purusha. This term in the Yoga and Samkhya traditions is the equivalent of "Atman" in Vedanta.

8 By the power of your Self: "God-realization is a unique state of consciousness. It is different from all the other states of consciousness because all the other states of consciousness are experienced through the medium of the individual mind; whereas the state of God-consciousness is in no way dependent upon the individual mind or any other medium. A medium is necessary for knowing something other than one's own self. For knowing one's own self, no medium is necessary" (Meher Baba).

9 Each "aspect of My glory" (*vibhuti*, manifestation) enumerated in 10.19–42 is a representative of its class in which the divine power reaches its height and is especially apparent. But God's all-pervading presence is not limited to the "best" forms; he manifests in all the opposites of existence while being beyond them, for "the Godhead is infinitely greater than any natural manifestation can be" (Aurobindo). The opposites of good and bad are nonexistent for those who are God-Realized; "it remains true, however, that the way to divinity lies through the renunciation of evil in favor of good" (Meher Baba).

10 Of all creative Powers I am the Creator: literally, "Of Adityas (solar deities) I am Vishnu." The god Vishnu originated in the Vedas as a sun deity. Later he emerged as a principal aspect of God, one of the Hindu trinity along with Brahma the Creator and Shiva the Destroyer. Vishnu is the Preserver, the personification of mercy. His devotees (called Vaishnavas) worship him as the supreme Lord, the source of all things; hence he is Creator as well.

the power of discrimination, which leads them to Me.

11 By My grace, I live in their hearts; and I dispel the darkness of ignorance by the shining light of wisdom.

Arjuna asked:

12 You are the Supreme Spirit,[6] the Eternal Home, the Holiest of the Holy, the Eternal Divine Self,[7] the Primal God, the Unborn, and the Omnipresent.

13 So have said the seers and the divine sage Narada; as well as Asita, Devala, and Vyasa; and You Yourself also say it.

14 I believe in what You have said, my Lord! For neither the godly nor the godless comprehend Your manifestation.

15 You alone know Yourself, by the power of Your Self;[8] you the Supreme Spirit, the Source and Master of all being, the Lord of Lords, the Ruler of the Universe.

16 Please tell me all about Your glorious manifestations, by means of which You pervade the world.

17 O Master! How shall I, by constant meditation, know You? My Lord! What are Your various manifestations through which I am to meditate on You?

18 Tell me again, I pray, about the fullness of Your power and Your glory; for I feel that I am never satisfied when I listen to Your immortal words.

Lord Shri Krishna replied:

19 So be it, My beloved friend! I will unfold to you some of the chief aspects of My glory.[9] Of its full extent there is no end.

20 O Arjuna! I am the Self, seated in the hearts of all beings; I am the beginning and the life, and I am the end of them all.

21 Of all creative Powers I am the Creator,[10] of luminaries the Sun; the

12 I am the Electric Force in the Powers of Nature: a reference to Indra, lord of rain, thunder, and lightning. Feuerstein refers to Indra as "a spiritual power granting flashes of inner illumination."

13 Of the senses I am the Mind: According to the Samkhya philosophy, there are eleven sense organs *(indriyas)*. The five organs of perception (eyes, ears, nose, tongue, skin) and the five organs of action (hands, feet, larynx, anus, genitals) serve to connect the manifest world with the eleventh organ, the mind *(manas,* or "lower mind").

14 Mount Meru, the sacred mountain at the center of the universe, is the abode of the gods.

15 Silent prayer: *japa*, the mental repetition of a mantra or a divine name in prayer or meditation.

16 Kapila: founder of the Samkhya school of philosophy.

17 Pegasus: literally, Uchchaihshrava, Indra's horse, born of nectar.

18 Thunderbolt: the *vajra*, Indra's magical weapon, which has been described in the scriptures as a hard, sharp metal instrument. Symbolically it is the destroyer of delusion.

19 Passion: Kama, god of desire, who represents "the first awakening desire of the One Spirit to become many" (Yogananda).

20 Father of fathers: the reference is to Aryaman, in Vedic mythology the chief of the departed ancestors who inhabit the nether regions.

21 Heathen: The Sanskrit word used here is *daityas*, demons at war with the gods. Prahlada was a *daitya* prince who turned to the worship of Vishnu and became a model of devotion.

22 Rama, like Krishna, was a divine incarnation, or Avatar. His story is told in the epic known as the *Ramayana,* in which he defeats the armies of the demon king Ravana, who had abducted Rama's wife, Sita.

Whirlwind among the winds, and the Moon among planets.

22 Of the Vedas I am the Hymns; I am the Electric Force[12] in the Powers of Nature; of the senses I am the Mind;[13] and I am the Intelligence in all that lives.

23 Among Forces of Vitality I am the Life; I am Mammon to the heathen and the godless; I am the Energy in fire, earth, wind, sky, heaven, sun, moon, and planets; and among mountains I am the Mount Meru.[14]

24 Among the priests, know, O Arjuna! that I am the Apostle Brihaspati, of generals I am Skanda the Commander-in-Chief, and of waters I am the Ocean.

25 Of the great seers I am Bhrigu, of words I am OM; of offerings I am the silent prayer,[15] among things immovable I am the Himalayas.

26 Of trees I am the sacred fig tree, of the divine seers Narada, of the heavenly singers I am Chitraratha, their leader, and of sages I am Kapila.[16]

27 Know that among horses I am Pegasus,[17] the heaven-born; among the lordly elephants I am the White One, and I am the Ruler among men.

28 I am the Thunderbolt[18] among weapons; of cows I am the Cow of Plenty, I am Passion[19] in those who procreate, and I am the Cobra among serpents.

29 I am the King Python among snakes, I am the Aqueous Principle among those that live in water; I am the Father of fathers,[20] and among rulers I am Death.

30 And I am the devotee Prahlada among the heathen;[21] of Time I am the Eternal Present; I am the Lion among beasts, and the Eagle among birds.

31 I am the Wind among the purifiers, the King Rama[22] among warriors, I am the Crocodile among the fishes, and I am the Ganges among the rivers.

23 | The copulative in compound words: an element of Sanskrit grammar called *dvandva*. Its significance is that in the joining of two or more words, the independent meaning of the individual words is preserved.

24 | I am Fame…: The original Sanskrit reads, "Among the feminine I am Fame." The seven nouns mentioned, all grammatically classified as feminine, can also be seen as "goddesses who are the powers of the Lord" (Ramanuja).

25 | Gayatri: an important meter in Vedic verses. Gayatri is also the name of a special mantra, drawn from the *Rig Veda*, which is said to be capable of conferring God-realization on one who practices it.

26 | Gambling of the cheat: God is the essence of everything, both good and bad. If Krishna chose to cheat at gambling, he would be the greatest of cheaters. "His greatness is not simply one-sided—it is all-sided" (Bhaktivedanta).

27 | "The scepter of rulers" signifies their power or "clout."

28 | The Silence of mystery: "God's silent presence within all phenomena of the cosmic dream is His best-kept secret" (Yogananda).

29 | No creature moving or unmoving: nothing that exists, whether animate or inanimate.

30 | Verses 41–42: God is everywhere and in everything, but also beyond everywhere and everything; all that exists is only a fraction of his infinite being. The Gita's teaching is neither pure pantheism (God *is* the manifest universe) nor theism (God is transcendent, beyond the world), but panentheism (God is both manifest and unmanifest, immanent and transcendent). The philosophy of Advaita (nondualistic) Vedanta affirms that God *appears* as this world, but is not this world. "He is not matter, but whatever is real in matter is He" (Vivekananda). Edgerton calls the Gita's teaching "frankly monotheistic" (emphasizing a personal God in the approachable form of the Avatar), even though some passages are monistic (emphasizing the absolute unity of Reality).

32 I am the Beginning, the Middle, and the End in creation; among sciences, I am the science of Spirituality; I am the Discussion among disputants.

33 Of letters I am A; I am the copulative[23] in compound words; I am Time inexhaustible; and I am the all-pervading Preserver.

34 I am all-devouring Death; I am the Origin of all that shall happen; I am Fame,[24] Fortune, Speech, Memory, Intellect, Constancy, and Forgiveness.

35 Of hymns I am Brihatsama, of meters I am Gayatri,[25] among the months I am Margashirsha (December), and I am the Spring among seasons.

36 I am the Gambling of the cheat,[26] and the Splendor of the splendid; I am Victory; I am Effort; and I am the Purity of the pure.

37 I am Shri Krishna among the Vrishni clan, and Arjuna among the Pandavas; of the saints I am Vyasa, and I am the Shukracharya among the sages.

38 I am the Scepter of rulers,[27] the Strategy of the conquerors, the Silence of mystery,[28] the Wisdom of the wise.

39 I am the Seed of all being, O Arjuna! No creature moving or unmoving[29] can live without Me.

40 O Arjuna! The aspects of My divine life are endless. I have mentioned but a few by way of illustration.

41 Whatever is glorious, excellent, beautiful, and mighty, be assured that it comes from a fragment of My splendor.

42 But what is the use of all these details to you? O Arjuna! I sustain this universe with only a small part of Myself.[30]

☑ In this climactic chapter of the Gita, Arjuna is given an overpowering vision *(darshana)* of Krishna's Infinite Being in what the poet Stephen Mitchell calls "one of the great moments in world literature." Arjuna's vision was cited as a universal example of religious experience by the Christian theologian Rudolf Otto, who coined the word "numinous" to characterize such experiences, in which there is an unsettling sense of one's own nothingness in the presence of the Divine. Arjuna beholds in Krishna a *mysterium tremendum et fascinans*—a Latin phrase used by Otto to signify a "terrifying and fascinating mystery" that overwhelms with awe and dread, yet at the same time charms and attracts. (See Aurobindo's comments below, n. 15.)

In order to give Arjuna this cosmic vision, Krishna temporarily awakens his divine sight, or spiritual "third eye" (see ch. 5, n. 13). But this dramatic glimpse, in which Arjuna perceives himself as separate from Krishna, is not the same as God-Realization, wherein one loses the sense of individual existence and experiences unity with God. Arjuna's cosmic vision is accompanied by fear, whereas union with God—the goal for which all of life has sprung into existence—is said to be an experience of ever-renewing bliss.

11 □ The Cosmic Vision

Arjuna said:

1 My Lord! Your words concerning the Supreme Secret of Self, given for my blessing, have dispelled the illusions which surrounded me.

2 O Lord! Whose eyes are like the lotus petal! You have described in detail the origin and the dissolution of being, and Your own Eternal Majesty.

3 I believe all as You have declared it. I long now to have a vision of Your Divine Form, O You Most High!

4 If You think that it can be made possible for me to see it, show me, O Lord of Lords! Your own Eternal Self.

Lord Shri Krishna replied:

5 Behold, O Arjuna! my celestial forms, by hundreds and thousands, various in kind, in color, and in shape.

6 Behold the Powers of Nature: fire, earth, wind, and sky; the sun, the heavens, the moon, the stars; all the forces of vitality and of healing; and the roving winds. See the myriad wonders revealed to none but you.

7 Here, in Me living as one, O Arjuna! behold the whole universe, movable and immovable, and anything else that you would see.

8 Yet since with mortal eyes you cannot see Me, lo! I give you the Divine Sight. See now the glory of My Sovereignty.

Sanjaya continued:

9 Having thus spoken, O King! The Lord Shri Krishna, the Almighty

[1] Although Krishna grants Arjuna's request for a vision of his divine form, some commentators emphasize that such miraculous experiences are not the goal of spiritual life. Srila Prabhupada, for example, points out that the close devotees and companions of Krishna were indifferent to displays of mystical power, because their attention was focused solely on their Divine Beloved. They loved him because he was intrinsically lovable, not for any mystical experience or blessing he might grant them.

[2] Progenitor: Brahma, the Creator (not to be confused with Brahman, the Absolute).

[3] Shining angels: literally, divine or celestial serpents *(uraga divya)*. Yogananda identifies the celestial serpents as the "creative forces that have their origin in the *kundalini*, the coiled life energy in the base center of the spine."

[4] The discus *(chakra,* "wheel") is an ancient Indian weapon, and Krishna's favorite. It had a hole in the center and was usually twirled rapidly around the finger and then hurled.

Prince of Wisdom, showed to Arjuna the Supreme Form of the Great God.[1]

10 There were countless eyes and mouths, and mystic forms innumerable, with shining ornaments and flaming celestial weapons.

11 Crowned with heavenly garlands, clothed in shining garments, anointed with divine unctions, He showed Himself as the Resplendent One, Marvelous, Boundless, Omnipresent.

12 Could a thousand suns blaze forth together, it would be but a faint reflection of the radiance of the Lord God.

13 In that vision Arjuna saw the universe, with its manifold shapes, all embraced in One, its Supreme Lord.

14 Thereupon Arjuna, dumb with awe, his hair on end, his head bowed, his hands clasped in salutation, addressed the Lord thus:

Arjuna said:

15 O Almighty God! I see in You the powers of Nature, the various Creatures of the world, the Progenitor[2] on his lotus throne, the Sages, and the shining angels.[3]

16 I see You, infinite in form, with, as it were, faces, eyes, and limbs everywhere; no beginning, no middle, no end; O Lord of the Universe, whose Form is universal!

17 I see You with the crown, the scepter, and the discus;[4] a blaze of splendor. Scarce can I gaze on You, so radiant You are, glowing like the blazing fire, brilliant as the sun, immeasurable.

18 Imperishable are You, the Sole One worthy to be known, the priceless Treasure-house of the universe, the immortal Guardian of the Life Eternal, the Spirit Everlasting.

19 Without beginning, without middle, and without end, infinite in power,

5 Folded palms: palms joined in a gesture of reverence known as *anjali mudra*. Modern Hindus use this gesture, with the palms held at the level of the heart, as a greeting (known as *namaskar*), which signifies, "The Divine in me greets the Divine within you." "When greeting a spiritual personage, the palms are held at eye level, and when making reverent salutation to a deity or the Divine, they are held above the head" (Feuerstein).

6 Great Seers: *maharishis*.

7 Adepts: *siddhas*. A *siddha* is "one who has succeeded" and is often known for supernatural powers.

8 Vital Forces: minor deities and celestial beings.

9 Fathers: spirits of the dead; ancestors.

10 Mammon-worshipers: *yakshas* (ghostlike beings, sometimes benevolent, sometimes not) and *asuras* (demons who are antigods).

Your arms all-embracing, the sun and moon Your eyes, Your face beaming with the fire of sacrifice, flooding the whole universe with light.

20 Alone You fill all the quarters of the sky, earth, and heaven, and the regions between. O Almighty Lord! Seeing Your marvelous and awe-inspiring Form, the spheres tremble with fear.

21 The troops of celestial Beings enter into You, some invoking You in fear, with folded palms;[5] the Great Seers[6] and Adepts[7] sing hymns to Your Glory, saying "All Hail."

22 The Vital Forces,[8] the Major Stars, Fire, Earth, Air, Sky, Sun, Heaven, Moon, and Planets; the Angels, the Guardians of the Universe, the divine Healers, the Winds, the Fathers,[9] the Heavenly Singers; and hosts of Mammon-worshipers,[10] demons as well as saints, are amazed.

23 Seeing Your stupendous Form, O Most Mighty! with its myriad faces, its innumerable eyes and limbs and terrible jaws, I myself and all the worlds are overwhelmed with awe.

24 When I see You, touching the Heavens, glowing with color, with open mouth and wide-open fiery eyes, I am terrified. O my Lord! my courage and my peace of mind desert me.

25 When I see Your mouths with their fearful jaws like glowing fires at the dissolution of creation, I lose all sense of place; I find no rest. Be merciful, O Lord in whom this universe abides!

26 All these sons of Dhritarashtra, with the hosts of princes, Bhishma, Drona, and Karna, as well as the other warrior chiefs belonging to our side;

27 I see them all rushing headlong into Your mouths, with terrible tusks, horrible to behold. Some are mangled between Your jaws, with their heads crushed to atoms.

28 As rivers in flood surge furiously to the ocean, so these heroes, the greatest among men, fling themselves into Your flaming mouths.

11 This verse brings to mind a famous episode in history, the first atomic bomb test, at Alamogordo, New Mexico, on July 16, 1945. Robert Oppenheimer—the scientist in charge of the Manhattan Project, which built the bomb—described how, in the solemn moments after the detonation, he recalled this verse, which he knew in another translation: "Now I am become Death, the destroyer of worlds." The word used in the original Sanskrit is *kala,* which can mean either Death or Time (since Time devours all creatures). "Destruction is always a simultaneous or alternate element which keeps pace with creation, and it is by destroying and renewing that the Master of Life does his long work of preservation" (Aurobindo).

12 "By this Krishna meant that the death of Arjuna's antagonists…was karmically ordained, and that Arjuna would only be an instrument in carrying out the divine law" (Yogananda).

@ "Krishna, as the Avatar, was not only spiritually perfect but Perfection personified. He was also perfect in everything. If He had wanted to, He could have shown Himself as a perfect drunkard, a perfect sinner, a perfect rogue, or a perfect murderer; but that would have shocked the world. Though possessed of perfection in every respect, it was not necessary for Him to exhibit it in fulfilling His mission…. Krishna proved to Arjuna, who was His devotee, that His apparent bringing about of the physical and mental annihilation of the vicious Kauravas was for their spiritual salvation. Perfection might manifest itself through killing or saving according to the spiritual demands of the situation."
—Meher Baba

@ "The Self is universal: so all actions will go on whether you strain yourself to be engaged in them or not. The work will go on of itself. Thus Krishna told Arjuna that he need not trouble to kill the Kauravas; they were already slain by God. It was not for him to resolve to work and worry himself about it, but to allow his own nature to carry out the will of the Higher Power."
—Ramana Maharshi

29 As moths fly impetuously to the flame, only to be killed, so these men rush into Your mouths to court their own destruction.

30 You seem to swallow up the worlds, to lap them in flame. Your glory fills the universe. Your fierce rays beat down upon it irresistibly.

31 Tell me then who You are that wear this dreadful Form. I bow before You, O Mighty One! Have mercy, I pray, and let me see You as You were at first. I do not know what You intend.

Lord Shri Krishna replied:

32 I have shown Myself to you as the Destroyer who lays waste the world, and whose purpose now is destruction.[11] In spite of your efforts, all these warriors gathered for battle shall not escape death.

33 Then gird up your loins, and conquer. Subdue your foes and enjoy the kingdom in prosperity. I have already doomed them. Be My instrument, Arjuna![12]

34 Drona and Bhishma, Jayadratha, and Karna, and other brave warriors— I have condemned them all. Destroy them; fight and fear not. Your foes shall be crushed.

Sanjaya continued:

35 Having heard these words from the Lord Shri Krishna, the Prince Arjuna, with folded hands trembling, prostrated himself and with choking voice, bowing down again and again, and overwhelmed with awe, once more addressed the Lord.

Arjuna said:

36 My Lord! It is natural that the world revels and rejoices when it sings the praises of Your glory; the demons fly in fear and the saints offer You their salutations.

37 How should they do otherwise? O Supremest Self, greater than the Powers of creation, the First Cause, Infinite, the Lord of Lords, the

13 The "Father" is Prajapati, an aspect of Brahma, the Creator. Shankara says that "Grandfather" means the father even of Brahma. "Father and Grandfather" may be understood as the primal ancestors of humanity.

14 Yadava: "descendant of Yadu," an ancient king.

15 "The hidden truth behind these terrifying forms is a reassuring, a heartening and delightful truth. There is something that makes the heart of the world to rejoice and take pleasure in the name and nearness of the Divine. It is the profound sense of that which makes us see in the dark face of Kali the face of the Mother and to perceive even in the midst of destruction the protecting arms of the Friend of creatures" (Aurobindo).

16 Krishna's divine form as Vishnu, cherished by Arjuna, has four hands, holding a conch, a scepter, a discus, and a lotus. Another distinctive feature of Krishna's form as seen in traditional art is his blue skin, representing "the color of his aura when he manifests" (Aurobindo). Blue is a symbol of spiritual infinity.

Home of the universe, Imperishable, Being and Not-Being, yet transcending both.

38 You are the Primal God, the Ancient, the Supreme Abode of this universe, the Knower, the Knowledge, and the Final Home. You fill everything. Your form is infinite.

39 You are the Wind, You are Death, You are the Fire, the Water, the Moon, the Father and the Grandfather.[13] Honor and glory to You a thousand and a thousand times! Again and again, salutation be to You, O my Lord!

40 Salutations to You in front and on every side, You who encompass me round about. Your power is infinite; Your majesty immeasurable; You uphold all things; yea, You Yourself are All.

41 Whatever I have said unto You in rashness, taking You only for a friend and addressing you as "O Krishna! O Yadava![14] O Friend!" in thoughtless familiarity, not understanding Your greatness;

42 Whatever insult I have offered to You in jest, in sport, or in repose, in conversation or at the banquet, alone or in a multitude, I ask Your forgiveness for them all, O You who are without an equal!

43 For You are the Father of all things movable and immovable, the Worshipful, the Master of Masters! In all the worlds there is none equal to You; how then superior; O You who stand alone, Supreme.

44 Therefore I prostrate myself before you, O Lord! Most Adorable! I salute You, I ask Your blessing. Only You can be trusted to bear with me, as father to son, as friend to friend, as lover to his beloved.

45 I rejoice that I have seen what never man saw before; yet, O Lord! I am overwhelmed with fear. Please take again the Form I know. Be merciful, O Lord! You who are the Home of the whole universe.[15]

46 I long to see You as You were before, with the crown, the scepter, and the discus in Your hands; in Your other Form, with Your four hands,[16]

@ As Krishna resumes his familiar human form in a compassionate response to Arjuna's plea, he broaches the subject of the next chapter: the path of love, or *bhakti yoga*. The last few verses of chapter 11 suggest that devotional love is not born of either extraordinary experiences or conventional religious activities, but rather thrives in a natural atmosphere of intimate companionship between lover and Beloved. The term *bhakti* comes from a Sanskrit word meaning "to share" and implies a reciprocal love shared by both God and the devotee. The relationship between Krishna and Arjuna is a model of this kind of love, which culminates in the spiritual emancipation of the devotee.

17 "The very heart, the quintessence, of the doctrines of the Gita is declared by Hindu commentators to be found in this verse" (Edgerton).

O You whose arms are countless and whose forms are infinite.

Lord Shri Krishna replied:

47 My beloved friend! It is only through My grace and power that you have been able to see this vision of splendor, the Universal, the Infinite, the Original. Never has it been seen by any but you.

48 Not by study of the scriptures, not by sacrifice or gift, not by ritual or rigorous austerity, is it possible for man on earth to see what you have seen, O foremost hero of the Kuru clan!

49 Be not afraid or bewildered by the terrible vision. Put away your fear and, with joyful mind, see Me once again in My usual Form.

Sanjaya continued:

50 Having thus spoken to Arjuna, Lord Shri Krishna showed Himself again in His accustomed form; and the Mighty Lord, in gentle tones, softly consoled him who lately trembled with fear.

Arjuna said:

51 Seeing You in Your gentle human form, my Lord, I am myself again, calm once more.

Lord Shri Krishna replied:

52 It is hard to see this vision of Me that you have seen. Even the most powerful have longed for it in vain.

53 Not by study of the scriptures, or by austerities, not by gifts or sacrifices, is it possible to see Me as you have done.

54 Only by tireless devotion can I be seen and known; only thus can a man become one with Me, O Arjuna!

55 He whose every action is done for My sake, to whom I am the final goal, who loves Me only and hates no one—O my dearest Son! Only he can realize Me.[17]

@ "An intense search after one's own reality is *bhakti*." —Shankara

1 Professor Edgerton thinks that the Gita recommends the "easy way" to salvation in order to appeal to the masses. Meher Baba suggests a deeper reason why love for the personal aspect of God is less difficult than worship of the Absolute: "there is no sense of effort because it is spontaneous." But surrendering one's actions to God out of love is not simple, for "love cannot be born of mere determination; through the exercise of will, one can at best be dutiful. One may, through struggle and effort, succeed in securing that his external action is in conformity with his conception of what is right; but such action is spiritually barren because it lacks the inward beauty of spontaneous love." Action, therefore, must be based on "the best intuitions of the heart."

2 "What man would not feel afraid in an ocean? It is no wonder then that My devotees should feel overcome with fear. O Arjuna, this is why I have become incarnate and come quickly to them. Those who were unattached I told to meditate on Me. To those with families, I recommended the repetition of My names. With My many names as boats in the ocean of worldly life, I have become the ferryman. With My love bound to them like a safety raft, I have led them to the other shore of liberation" (Jnanadeva).

12 □ The Path of Love: Bhakti Yoga

Arjuna asked:

1 My Lord! Which are the better devotees who worship You, those who try to know You as a Personal God or those who worship You as Impersonal and Indestructible?

Lord Shri Krishna replied:

2 Those who keep their minds fixed on Me, who worship Me always with unwavering faith and concentration—these are the very best.

3 Those who worship Me as the Indestructible, the Undefinable, the Unmanifest, the Omnipresent, the Unthinkable, the Primeval, the Immutable, and the Eternal;

4 Subduing their senses, viewing all conditions of life with the same eye, and working for the welfare of all beings, assuredly they come to Me.

5 But they who thus fix their attention on the Absolute and Impersonal encounter greater hardships; for it is difficult for those who possess a body to realize Me as without one.[1]

6 Verily, those who surrender their actions to Me, who muse on Me, worship Me, and meditate on Me alone, with no thought save of Me,

7 O Arjuna! I rescue them quickly from the ocean of life and death,[2] for their minds are fixed on Me.

8 Then let your mind cling only to Me, let your intellect abide in Me; and without doubt you shall live hereafter in Me alone.

[@] "When love is deep and intense, it is called *bhakti*, or devotion. In its initial stages devotion is expressed through symbol worship, supplication before the deities, reverence and allegiance to the revealed scriptures, or the pursuit of the Highest through abstract thinking. In its more advanced stages devotion expresses itself as interest in human welfare and the service of humanity, love and reverence for saints, and allegiance and obedience to a spiritual Master. Love for a living Perfect Master is a unique stage of devotion, for it eventually gets transformed into *para-bhakti*, or divine love." —Meher Baba

[3] Constant practice: "Practice consists in withdrawing the thought from all objects and fixing it, again and again, on one ideal" (Nikhilananda).

[4] Self-centered: that is, centered in the Self. "In the palace of his heart, the individual self and the Supreme are seated together in splendor" (Jnanadeva).

[5] "He who does not harm the world, and whom the world cannot harm": Sargeant translates this as "He from whom the world does not shrink, and who does not shrink from the world."

[6] Renounces all initiative: "He habitually renounces all actions calculated to secure the objects of enjoyment, whether of this world or of the next. He has abandoned all egoistic, personal and mental initiative in all actions, mental and physical. He has merged his will in the cosmic will. He allows the divine will to work through him" (Sivananda).

[7] No fixed abode: "When the chrysalis is broken, the butterfly goes out freely to enjoy the sunshine and flowers. So, when the sense of individuality is merged in the Infinite Consciousness of the Lord, symbolized by Shri Krishna or Rama, that higher Consciousness of freedom and detachment blossoms forth, and the whole world becomes a home to the devotee" (Shastri).

9 But if you cannot fix your mind firmly on Me, then, My beloved friend! try to do so by constant practice.[3]

10 And if you are not strong enough to practice concentration, then devote yourself to My service, do all your acts for My sake, and you shall still attain the goal.

11 And if you are too weak even for this, then seek refuge in union with Me, and with perfect self-control renounce the fruit of all your action.

12 Knowledge is superior to blind action, meditation to mere knowledge, renunciation of the fruit of action to meditation, and where there is renunciation, peace will follow.

13 He who is incapable of hatred toward any being, who is kind and compassionate, free from selfishness, without pride, equable in pleasure and in pain, and forgiving,

14 Always contented, self-centered,[4] self-controlled, resolute, with mind and reason dedicated to Me, such a devotee of Mine is my beloved.

15 He who does not harm the world, and whom the world cannot harm,[5] who is not carried away by any impulse of joy, anger, or fear, such a one is My beloved.

16 He who expects nothing, who is pure, watchful, indifferent, unruffled, and who renounces all initiative,[6] such a one is My beloved.

17 He who is beyond joy and hate, who neither laments nor desires, to whom good and evil fortunes are the same, such a one is My beloved.

18 He to whom friend and foe are alike, who welcomes equally honor and dishonor, heat and cold, pleasure and pain, who is enamored of nothing,

19 Who is indifferent to praise and censure, who enjoys silence, who is contented with every fate, who has no fixed abode,[7] who is steadfast in mind and filled with devotion, such a one is My beloved.

8 My most beloved: God loves all beings equally (see 9.29); but, as Aurobindo says, there is also a personal relation of the Divine to the human being in which He is especially close to the person who comes near to Him.

@ "A true devotee loves the Lord for love's sake. There is no bargaining or shopkeeping in his love. He does not even seek liberation, though, in spite of himself, he becomes liberated."

—Swami Prabhavananda

@ "Anyone who has perceived the Self through the intellect cannot help adoring the Self. Therefore the yoga of *bhakti* or devotion is not incompatible with the yoga of intellect." —Gita comic book

20 Verily those who love the spiritual wisdom as I have taught, whose faith never fails, and who concentrate their whole nature on Me, they indeed are My most beloved.[8]

@ The first, unnumbered verse of chapter 13 is omitted from many editions of the Gita.

1 Playground: literally, the field *(kshetra)*. "The body is called 'field' because the fruits of action are reaped in it as in a field, or because it is subject to decay" (Nikhilananda). Other translations title this chapter "The Field and the Knower of the Field." The field signifies matter or Nature; the knower of the field is Spirit.

2 Out of the primal material nature first evolves the intellect *(buddhi)*, then the "personality" *(ahamkara*, ego or sense of "I"), then the lower mind *(manas)*, which mediates between the ego and the ten sense organs (see diagram on page 106). The five sense organs (ears, eyes, skin, tongue, and nose) are linked respectively in experience to the five elements (space, fire, air, water, and earth) through the corresponding five senses (hearing, sight, touch, taste, and smell).

"Mysterious life-force" is *avyakta*, the unmanifest, undifferentiated nature, which is the source of manifest forms. (The term *prakriti* can mean both manifest and unmanifest nature.) According to Shankara, this life-force is the creative energy *(shakti)* of the Lord, equated with Maya (see 7.14).

13 □ Matter and Spirit

Arjuna asked:

My Lord! Who is God and what is Nature; what is Matter and what is the Self; what is that they call Wisdom, and what is it that is worth knowing? I wish to have this explained.

Lord Shri Krishna replied:

1 O Arjuna! The body of man is the playground[1] of the Self; and that which knows the activities of Matter, sages call the Self.

2 I am the Omniscient Self that abides in the playground of Matter; knowledge of Matter and of the all-knowing Self is wisdom.

3 What is called Matter, of what it is composed, whence it came, and why it changes, what the Self is, and what Its power—this I will now briefly set forth.

4 Seers have sung of It in various ways, in many hymns and sacred Vedic songs, weighty in thought and convincing in argument.

5 The five great fundamentals (earth, fire, air, water, and ether), personality, intellect, the mysterious life force, the ten organs of perception and action, the mind and the five domains of sensation;[2]

6 Desire, aversion, pleasure, pain, sympathy, vitality, and the persistent clinging to life, these are in brief the constituents of changing Matter.

7 Humility, sincerity, harmlessness, forgiveness, rectitude, service of the Master, purity, steadfastness, self-control;

8 Renunciation of the delights of sense, absence of pride, right under-

The Twenty-four Principles of Nature
According to the Samkhya Philosophy

PURUSHA *(Spirit)*

(1) PRAKRITI
(Nature)
↓
(2) BUDDHI
(intellect, discriminative intelligence)
↓
(3) AHAMKARA
(ego, "I"-consciousness)
↓
(4) MANAS
(mind, organ of thought)
↓

↓	↓	↓	↓
(5–9)	**(10–14)**	**(15–19)**	**(20–24)**
ORGANS OF PERCEPTION	& ACTION	SUBTLE ELEMENTS	GROSS ELEMENTS
hearing	speech	sound	ether (space)
skin	grasping	touch	air
eyes	walking	form	fire
tongue	reproduction	taste	water
nose	elimination	smell	earth

3 Neither with form nor without it: literally, neither being *(sat)* nor non-being *(asat)*. The existence of God cannot be limited to one pole of a pair of opposites, because God transcends all opposites. "It is meaningless to say that He is or is not. It is impossible to attain Him through thought" (Jnanadeva).

4 The Light of lights: a phrase from the Upanishads. Ramanuja comments that the effulgence of the Self alone is what illumines the sun and moon, lamps, gems, and all other lights.

standing of the painful problems of birth and death, of age and sickness;

9 Indifference; nonattachment to sex, progeny, or home; equanimity in good fortune and in bad;

10 Unswerving devotion to Me, by concentration on Me and Me alone, a love for solitude, indifference to social life;

11 Constant yearning for the knowledge of Self, and pondering over the lessons of the great Truth—this is Wisdom, all else ignorance.

12 I will speak to you now of that great Truth which man ought to know, since by its means he will win immortal bliss; That which is without beginning, the Eternal Spirit which dwells in Me, neither with form nor yet without it.³

13 Everywhere are Its hands and Its feet, everywhere It has eyes that see, heads that think, and mouths that speak; everywhere It listens; It dwells in all the worlds; It envelops them all.

14 Beyond the senses, It yet shines through every sense perception. Bound to nothing, It yet sustains everything. Unaffected by the Qualities, It still enjoys them all.

15 It is within all beings, yet outside; motionless yet moving; too subtle to be perceived; far away yet always near.

16 In all beings undivided, yet living in division, It is the upholder of all, Creator and Destroyer alike;

17 It is the Light of lights,⁴ beyond the reach of darkness; the Wisdom, the only thing that is worth knowing or that wisdom can teach; the Presence in the hearts of all.

18 Thus have I told you in brief what Matter is, and the Self worth realizing and what is Wisdom. He who is devoted to Me knows; and assuredly he will enter into Me.

5 In commenting on this verse, Sri Aurobindo says that there are two basic attitudes one can take toward Nature: (1) that of the pure Witness, utterly detached and free, which impersonally enjoys and observes but does not identify with the actions of Nature, and (2) that of the upholder and sustainer of Nature, supporting and conducting the "energy which unrolls the spectacle of the cosmos." The second attitude represents "an important step forward" toward identification with the divine joy of cosmic being.

6 By pure reason: literally, "by Samkhya yoga" (see ch. 2, n. 13). "Here *samkhya-yoga* stands for the spiritual practice of discernment *(viveka)* between the real and the unreal" (Feuerstein).

7 His actions do not mar his spiritual life: An alternative reading is "the self cannot injure the self" (Miller) or "he cannot harm the Self by the self" (Mitchell)—meaning that if we see the Self in all beings we do not hurt anyone, because to do so would be to hurt our own self in another form.

19 Know further that Nature and God have no beginning; and that differences of character and quality have their origin in Nature only.

20 Nature is the Law which generates cause and effect; God is the source of the enjoyment of all pleasure and pain.

21 God dwelling in the heart of Nature experiences the Qualities which Nature brings forth; and His affinity toward the Qualities is the reason for His living in a good or evil body.

22 Thus in the body of man dwells the Supreme God: He who sees and permits, upholds and enjoys; the Highest God and the Highest Self.

23 He who understands God and Nature[5] along with her Qualities, whatever be his condition in life, he comes not again to earth.

24 Some realize the Supreme by meditating, by its aid, on the Self within; others by pure reason,[6] others by right action.

25 Others, again, having no direct knowledge but only hearing from others, nevertheless worship, and they too, if true to the teachings, cross the sea of death.

26 Wherever life is seen in things movable or immovable, it is the joint product of Matter and Spirit.

27 He who can see the Supreme Lord in all beings, the Imperishable amid the perishable, he it is who really sees.

28 Beholding the Lord in all things equally, his actions do not mar his spiritual life[7] but lead him to the height of Bliss.

29 He who understands that it is only the Law of Nature that brings action to fruition, and that the Self never acts, alone knows the Truth.

30 He who sees the diverse forms of life all rooted in the One, and growing forth from Him, he shall indeed find the Absolute.

31 The Supreme Spirit, O Prince! is without beginning, without Qualities,

@ "Nature's task is done, this unselfish task which our sweet nurse, Nature, had imposed upon herself. She gently took the self-forgetting soul by the hand, as it were, and showed him all the experiences in the universe, all manifestations, bringing him higher and higher through various bodies, till his lost glory came back and he remembered his own nature. Then the kind mother went back the same way she came, for others who have also lost their way in the trackless desert of life. And thus is she working, without beginning and without end. And thus through pleasure and pain, through good and evil, the infinite river of souls is flowing into the ocean of perfection, of self-realization."

—Swami Vivekananda

and Imperishable, and though it be within the body, yet It does not act, nor is It affected by action.

32 As space, though present everywhere, remains by reason of its subtlety unaffected, so the Self, though present in all forms, retains Its purity unalloyed.

33 As the one Sun illuminates the whole earth, so the Lord illumines the whole universe.

34 Those who with the eyes of wisdom thus see the difference between Matter and Spirit, and know how to liberate Life from the Law of Nature, they attain the Supreme.

[1] The three Qualities—*sattva* (Purity), *rajas* (Passion), and *tamas* (Ignorance)—are first mentioned in chapter 2; see ch. 2, n. 17.

[@] "Three thieves fell upon a merchant who was on his way home and robbed him. Tamas wanted to kill the merchant in order to destroy any trace of the crime. The other two hesitated, and Rajas said, 'Let's tie him to a tree. Whether or not he is found will depend on his karma.' They bound him to a tree and hurried away. After a while, Sattva returned and cut the ropes. The merchant was overjoyed. 'You've saved my life,' he said. 'Come back to the village with me and I'll reward you.' 'No, that won't do,' replied Sattva. 'The police know me to be a thief. The only thing I could do was release you from your bonds.'"

—Parable of Ramakrishna, who adds, "Sattva is also a robber. It cannot give man the ultimate Knowledge of Truth, though it shows him the road leading to the Supreme Abode of God."

14 □ The Three Qualities

Lord Shri Krishna continued:

1   Now I will reveal unto you the Wisdom which is beyond knowledge, by attaining which the sages have reached Perfection.

2   Dwelling in Wisdom and realizing My Divinity, they are not born again when the universe is re-created at the beginning of every cycle, nor are they affected when it is dissolved.

3   The eternal Cosmos is My womb, in which I plant the seed from which all beings are born, O Prince!

4   O illustrious son of Kunti! Through whatever wombs men are born, it is the Spirit Itself that conceives, and I am their Father.

5   Purity, Passion, and Ignorance are the Qualities[1] which the Law of Nature brings forth. They fetter the free Spirit in all beings.

6   O Sinless One! Of these, Purity, being luminous, strong, and invulnerable, binds one by its yearning for happiness and illumination.

7   Passion, engendered by thirst for pleasure and attachment, binds the soul through its fondness for activity.

8   But Ignorance, the product of darkness, stupefies the senses in all embodied beings, binding them by the chains of folly, indolence, and lethargy.

9   Purity brings happiness, Passion commotion, and Ignorance, which obscures wisdom, leads to a life of failure.

10 O Prince! Purity prevails when Passion and Ignorance are overcome;

[2] Sri Easwaran suggests how one can overcome the Qualities: "The way to transform tamas into rajas is through activity. Then slowly we have to transform rajas into sattva; we must begin to direct all of our energies to the selfless service of those around us. We can harness our energy and restlessness and direct it to the supreme goal."

[3] "That which is beyond" the Qualities is God, who is ultimately the source of everything. "The enlightened perceive this, O Arjuna, just as a person who awakes from sleep realizes that he had a dream.... Just as an actor isn't deceived by the role that he's playing, in the same way, we should understand the qualities without identifying with them" (Jnanadeva).

[4] "When the pieces of a broken pot are thrown away, the space which was inside the pot is absorbed by the space outside. In the same way, if a person remembers his true nature, he experiences nothing but union, and awareness of the body passes away. Such a person has transcended the qualities, having attained enlightenment while still in the body" (Jnanadeva).

Passion, when Purity and Ignorance are overcome; and Ignorance when it overcomes Purity and Passion.**2**

11 When the light of knowledge gleams forth from all the gates of the body, then be sure that Purity prevails.

12 O best of Indians! Avarice, the impulse to act, and the beginning of action itself, are all due to the dominance of Passion.

13 Darkness, stagnation, folly, and infatuation are the result of the domination of Ignorance, O joy of the Kuru clan!

14 When Purity prevails, the soul on quitting the body passes on to the pure regions where live those who know the Highest.

15 When Passion prevails, the soul is reborn among those who love activity; when Ignorance rules, it enters the wombs of the ignorant.

16 They say the fruit of a meritorious action is spotless and full of Purity; the outcome of Passion is misery, and of Ignorance darkness.

17 Purity engenders Wisdom, Passion avarice, and Ignorance folly, infatuation, and darkness.

18 When Purity is in the ascendant, the man evolves; when Passion, he neither evolves nor degenerates; when Ignorance, he is lost.

19 As soon as a man understands that it is only the Qualities which act and nothing else, and perceives That which is beyond,**3** he attains My divine nature.

20 When the soul transcends the Qualities,**4** which are the real cause of physical existence, then, freed from birth and death, from old age and misery, he quaffs the nectar of immortality.

Arjuna asked:

21 My Lord! By what signs can he who has transcended the Qualities be recognized? How does he act? How does he live beyond them?

5 "The reason for acting with indifference is that actions cannot really affect the soul for good or ill; they concern matter exclusively" (Edgerton).

@ "Neither seek nor avoid: take what comes. This is freedom—to be affected by nothing. Do not merely endure; be unattached. Remember the story of the bull. A mosquito sat on the long horn of a certain bull. Then his conscience troubled him and he said: 'Mr. Bull, I have been sitting here a long time; perhaps I annoy you. I am sorry. I will go away.' But the bull replied: 'Oh no, not at all! Bring your whole family and live on my horn. What can you do to me?'"

—Swami Vivekananda

6 "A sleeping man doesn't care whether a snake or a heavenly nymph is lying near him. Similarly, these pairs of opposites don't affect the person who is united with God" (Jnanadeva).

Lord Shri Krishna replied:

22 O Prince! He who shuns not the Quality which is present, and longs not for that which is absent;

23 He who maintains an attitude of indifference,[5] who is not disturbed by the Qualities, who realizes that it is only they who act, and remains calm;

24 Who accepts pleasure or pain as it comes, is centered in his Self, to whom a piece of clay or a stone or gold are the same,[6] who neither likes nor dislikes, who is steadfast, indifferent alike to praise or censure;

25 Who looks equally upon honor and dishonor, loves friends and foes alike, abandons all initiative, such is he who transcends the Qualities.

26 And he who serves Me and only Me, with unfaltering devotion, shall overcome the Qualities, and become One with the Eternal.

27 For I am the Home of the Spirit, the continual Source of immortality, of eternal Righteousness, and of infinite Joy.

1 The image here is of a giant inverted tree with its roots in the air and its branches below. This symbolic tree, referred to in the scriptures as the *ashvattha*, is traditionally associated with the sacred fig tree *(ficus religiosa)*, known in India as the pipal. It is sacred to Buddhists as the bodhi tree, under which the Buddha attained enlightenment. Some commentators equate the *ashvattha* with the banyan *(ficus bengalensis)* because, like the fig, it has branches that reach down to root in the earth. As a symbol of cosmic manifestation or worldly existence *(samsara)*, the *ashvattha* is comparable to the Tree of Life. It is also an image of the human nervous system. The leaves are the sensory organs receiving knowledge of the phenomenal world (symbolized by "scriptures," or Vedas).

2 Never come back: "Once a salt doll went to measure the depth of the ocean. It wanted to tell others how deep the water was. But this is could never do, for no sooner did it get into the water than it melted. Now who was there to report the ocean's depth?" (Ramakrishna).

3 This verse states that the individual living soul *(jiva)* is an integral part of the Eternal Self. But how can the individual soul be a fragment of the Eternal Self yet also be considered identical with the one Self? Shankara likens the individual soul to "the sun reflected in water: the reflected sun is but a portion of the real sun; and on the removal of water, the reflected sun returns to the original sun and remains as that very sun." Thus, according to Shankara's teaching of nondualism, the "portioning" into individual souls is imaginary, since the One God cannot be divided in reality.

15 □ The Lord God

Lord Shri Krishna continued:

1 This phenomenal creation, which is both ephemeral and eternal, is like a tree, but having its seed above in the Highest, and its ramifications on this earth below.[1] The scriptures are its leaves, and he who understands this, knows.

2 Its branches shoot upward and downward, deriving their nourishment from the Qualities; its buds are the objects of sense; and its roots, which follow the Law causing man's regeneration and degeneration, pierce downward into the soil.

3 In this world its true form is not known, neither its origin nor its end, and its strength is not understood, until the tree with its roots striking deep into the earth is hewn down by the sharp axe of nonattachment.

4 Beyond lies the Path, from which, when found, there is no return. This is the Primal God from whence this ancient creation has sprung.

5 The wise attain Eternity when, freed from pride and delusion, they have conquered their love for the things of sense; when, renouncing desire and fixing their gaze on the Self, they have ceased to be tossed to and fro by the opposing sensations, like pleasure and pain.

6 Neither sun, moon, nor fire shine there. Those who go thither never come back.[2] For, O Arjuna! that is My Celestial Home.

7 It is only a very small part of My Eternal Self, which is the life of this universe,[3] drawing round itself the six senses, the mind the last, which have their source in Nature.

4 | The unintelligent *(achetasa):* other possible translations giving different shades of meaning include "thoughtless," "ignorant," "unperfected," and "unthinking."

5 | By My cool moonbeams...: Edgerton's literal translation reads: "Becoming the juicy *soma*, I make all plants to grow." *Soma* (literally "juice") is identified with the moon, which rules water and other fluids. The inner meaning of this passage is suggested by Yogananda: "Manifesting through the elemental principles of Nature or Prakriti ('the watery moon'), all forms ('plants'—offshoots) come into being as differentiated rays of the one creative light of God."

6 | The Supreme Personality: *purushottama*. Lord Krishna as the Avatar is the Highest of the High.

8 When the Supreme Lord enters a body or leaves it, He gathers these senses together and travels on with them, as the wind gathers perfume while passing through the flowers.

9 He is the perception of the ear, the eye, the touch, the taste, and the smell, yea and of the mind also; and the enjoyment of the things which they perceive is also His.

10 The ignorant do not see that it is He who is present in life and who departs at death or even that it is He who enjoys pleasure through the Qualities. Only the eye of wisdom sees.

11 The saints with great effort find Him within themselves; but not the unintelligent,[4] who in spite of every effort cannot control their minds.

12 Remember that the Light which, proceeding from the sun, illumines the whole world, and the Light which is in the moon, and that which is in the fire also, all are born of me.

13 I enter this world and animate all My creatures with My vitality; and by My cool moonbeams I nourish the plants.[5]

14 Becoming the fire of life, I pass into their bodies and, uniting with the vital streams of Prana and Apana, I digest the various kinds of food.

15 I am enthroned in the hearts of all; memory, wisdom, and discrimination owe their origin to Me. I am He who is to be realized in the scriptures; I inspire their wisdom and I know their truth.

16 There are two aspects in Nature: the perishable and the imperishable. All life in this world belongs to the former, the unchanging element belongs to the latter.

17 But higher than all am I, the Supreme God, the Absolute Self, the Eternal Lord, who pervades the worlds and upholds them all.

18 Beyond comparison of the Eternal with the non-eternal am I, Who am called by scriptures and sages the Supreme Personality,[6] the Highest God.

7 | Jnanadeva comments, "A person who worships Me isn't different from Me, just as waves aren't different from the sea." Krishna seems to suggest that true, wholehearted worship arises when the worshiper realizes his or her oneness with God, the object of worship.

19 He who with unclouded vision sees Me as the Lord God, knows all there is to be known, and always shall worship**7** Me with his whole heart.

20 Thus, O Sinless One! I have revealed to you this most mystic knowledge. He who understands gains wisdom, and attains the consummation of life.

1 Clean living: This phrase has also been translated as "purity of being," "purity of heart," and "purification of essence."

2 Candor *(arjava):* honesty, sincerity, or uprightness. Ramanuja defines uprightness as "oneness of thought, word, and deed in one's dealing with others." Honesty about oneself (not pretending to be what one is not) is especially important. As Meher Baba explains: "Infinite honesty is one of the aspects of God, and therefore the least hypocrisy in ourselves keeps us aloof from God."

3 Harmlessness: *ahimsa,* nonviolence. Pure nonviolence is the ideal, but many commentators acknowledge that there are exceptions. As noted by Gandhi, "*Ahimsa* also embraces violence deliberately committed out of compassion." This would include violence in defense of the innocent. The war that is the setting for the Gita is considered a just war, necessary to overcome evil forces and uphold the *dharma.*

4 Straightforwardness *(apaishuna):* also translated as "nonslanderousness," "aversion to fault-finding," "an unmalicious tongue," and "no backbiting." Meher Baba identifies backbiting as a disastrous habit, because it causes us to take on the bad impressions *(samskaras)* of those we are criticizing. "A true devotee, like a bee, sips the honey of good qualities from the hearts of his companions" (Yogananda).

5 Valor *(tejas,* "fire"): also translated as "radiance of character," "energy," "brilliance," or "vigor."

16 ☐ The Divine and Demoniac Civilizations

Lord Shri Krishna continued:

1 Fearlessness, clean living,**1** unceasing concentration on wisdom, readiness to give, self-control, a spirit of sacrifice, regular study of the scriptures, austerities, candor,**2**

2 Harmlessness,**3** truth, absence of wrath, renunciation, contentment, straightforwardness,**4** compassion toward all, uncovetousness, courtesy, modesty, constancy,

3 Valor,**5** forgiveness, fortitude, purity, freedom from hate and vanity; these are his who possesses the Godly Qualities, O Arjuna!

4 Hypocrisy, pride, insolence, cruelty, ignorance, belong to him who is born of the godless qualities.

5 Godly qualities lead to liberation; godless to bondage. Do not be anxious, Prince! You have the Godly qualities.

6 All beings are of two classes: Godly and godless. The Godly I have described; I will now describe the other.

7 The godless do not know how to act, or how to renounce. They have neither purity nor truth. They do not understand the right principles of conduct.

8 They say that the universe is an accident with no purpose and no God. Life is created by sexual union, a product of lust and nothing else.

9 Thinking thus, these degraded souls, these enemies of mankind—whose

6 According to several commentators, this verse does not imply that any soul is ever eternally damned. Shankara says that it means simply that those who fail to follow the way taught by Krishna will inevitably suffer (not as punishment for failing to follow his way, but because his way means release from suffering). As Aurobindo writes, "All souls are eternal portions of the Divine, the Asura as well as the Deva; all can come to salvation: even the greatest sinner can turn to the Divine."

@ "It must not be thought that the Lord has created some persons with evil tendencies in order to punish them. He is impartial—without any attachment or hatred for any created being. Only those whose sins, the result of their own evil action, have been destroyed feel His attraction. As a magnet exercises uniform attraction, He attracts all beings to Him. When the dirt of wickedness covering our soul is washed away by the tears of divine love, we become united with the Lord. Every soul will eventually realize God."   —Swami Nikhilananda

intelligence is negligible and whose deeds are monstrous—come into the world only to destroy.

10 Giving themselves up to insatiable passions, hypocritical, self-sufficient and arrogant, cherishing false conceptions founded on delusion, they work only to carry out their own unholy purposes.

11 Poring anxiously over evil resolutions, which only end in death; seeking only the gratification of desire as the highest goal; seeing nothing beyond;

12 Caught in the toils of a hundred vain hopes, the slaves of passion and of wrath, they accumulate hoards of unjust wealth, only to pander to their sensual desire.

13 "This have I gained today, tomorrow I will gratify another desire; this wealth is mine now, the rest shall be mine ere long;

14 "I have slain one enemy, I will slay the others also; I am worthy to enjoy, I am the Almighty, I am perfect, powerful, and happy;

15 "I am rich, I am well bred; who is there to compare with me? I will sacrifice, I will give, I will pay—and I will enjoy." Thus blinded by ignorance;

16 Perplexed by discordant thoughts, entangled in the snares of desire, infatuated by passion, they sink into the horrors of hell.

17 Self-conceited, stubborn, rich, proud, and insolent, they make a display of their patronage, disregarding the rules of decency.

18 Puffed up by power and inordinate conceit, swayed by lust and wrath, these wicked people hate Me who am within them, as I am within all.

19 Those who thus hate Me, who are cruel, the dregs of mankind, I condemn them to a continuous, miserable, and godless rebirth.

20 So reborn, they spend life after life enveloped in delusion. And they never reach Me, O Prince! but degenerate into still lower forms of life.[6]

7 Lust *(kama)* means desire for any object, for sensual pleasure, or for pleasurable experiences generally. "Lust, greed, and anger respectively have body, heart, and mind as their vehicles of expression" (Meher Baba). Yogananda points out that greed, lust, and anger are associated with the three lower chakras.

8 How to avoid them? "When you have thoughts of anger, lust, or greed, do not worry about them and do not try to check them. Let all such thoughts come and go without putting them into action. Try to think counter-thoughts in order to discern, to discriminate, to learn, and above all to unlearn the actions which are prompted by your own impressions" (Meher Baba).

9 "The intention of this verse is to tell us not to look upon ourselves as an authority, that is, not to be guided by our wishes and feelings.... Here Shri Krishna refers to the struggle in us between divine and demoniac impulses. So long as we are in that condition, we should be guided by the authority of the Shastras [scriptures]" (Gandhi). Once one has mastered the desire nature through self-control, one is "ready for a freer intelligent self-guidance and then for the highest supreme law and supreme liberty of the spiritual nature" (Aurobindo).

@ "Do you know the use of the scriptures? A man once wrote a letter to a relative, asking him to send five seers [roughly, kilograms] of sweetmeats and a piece of cloth. The relative received the letter, read it, and remembered about the sweetmeats and the cloth. Then he threw the letter away. Of what further use was it?"

—Ramakrishna

21 The gates of hell are three: lust, wrath, and avarice.**7** They destroy the Self. Avoid them.**8**

22 These are the gates which lead to darkness; if a man avoids them, he will ensure his own welfare and in the end will attain his liberation.

23 But he who neglects the commands of the scriptures and follows the promptings of passion, he does not attain perfection, happiness, or the final goal.

24 Therefore, whenever there is a doubt whether you should do a thing or not, let the scriptures guide your conduct.**9** In the light of the scriptures should you labor the whole of your life.

1 Arjuna's question might also be phrased: "What is the condition of those who worship with faith yet reject the scriptures?"

@ "'Faith' here is not a very adequate translation of *shraddha*, which means much more. Literally, *shraddha* is 'that which is placed in the heart': all the beliefs we hold so deeply that we never think to question them. It is the set of beliefs, values, prejudices, and prepossessions that colors our perceptions, governs our thinking, dictates our responses, and shapes our lives, generally without our even being aware of its presence and power."   —Eknath Easwaran

17 □ The Threefold Faith

Arjuna asked:

1 My Lord! Those who do acts of sacrifice, not according to the scriptures but nevertheless with implicit faith, what is their condition? Is it one of Purity, of Passion, or of Ignorance?[1]

Lord Shri Krishna replied:

2 Man has an inherent faith in one or other of the Qualities—Purity, Passion, and Ignorance. Now listen.

3 The faith of every man conforms to his nature. By nature he is full of faith. He is in fact what his faith makes him.

4 The Pure worship the true God; the Passionate, the powers of wealth and magic; the Ignorant, the spirits of the dead and of the lower orders of nature.

5 Those who practice austerities not commanded by scripture, who are slaves to hypocrisy and egotism, who are carried away by the fury of desire and passion,

6 They are ignorant. They torment the organs of the body; and they harass Me also, who lives within. Know that they are devoted to evil.

7 The food which men enjoy is also threefold, like the ways of sacrifice, austerity, and almsgiving. Listen to the distinction.

8 The foods that prolong life and increase purity, vigor, health, cheerfulness, and happiness are those that are delicious, soothing, substantial, and agreeable. These are loved by the Pure.

2 Ayurveda (traditional Indian medicine) recognizes six tastes: sweet, salty, sour, pungent, bitter, and astringent. "Sweet is the primary Sattvic [Pure] taste because it is nurturing and harmonizing, reflecting the energy of love…. However, we need all six tastes to various degrees. The right balance of tastes is itself Sattvic…. Too much of any taste becomes Tamasic or dulling" (Frawley).

3 Worship of God and the Master; respect for the preacher and the philosopher: Elsewhere translated as "reverence for the devas, the seers, the teachers, and the sages" (Prabhavananda & Isherwood) or "honoring gods, priests, teachers, and wise men" (Miller). Yogananda sums it up as "worshipful regard for divinity in its various manifestations."

4 Rectitude: *arjava*; see ch. 16, n. 2.

5 Continence: *brahmacharya*; see ch. 6, n. 9.

6 Speech that hurts no one, that is true: "It is not enough merely to tell the truth; one's words should also be sweet, healing, and beneficial to others" (Yogananda). "The truth when told is that which uplifts another. Anything which crushes another person cannot be true" (Meher Baba).

7 Constant study of the scriptures: *svadhyaya*, which is "more than mere intellectual learning. It approaches the quality of meditation" (Feuerstein). It includes the practice of chanting or reciting sacred texts. Yogananda says it also includes meditating on truths in the form of affirmations.

8 Silence (*mauna,* from the same root that forms the word *muni,* sage): The practice of silence has been recognized since ancient times as "a powerful means of inner development" (Feuerstein). However, silence of the mind may be more significant than the literal restraint of speech or sound. Yogananda interprets silence in this verse as "inner stillness," and Nikhilananda equates it with "control of thought, which precedes the silence of the tongue."

9 Those in whom Passion is dominant like foods that are bitter, sour, salt, over-hot, pungent, dry, and burning.[2] These produce unhappiness, repentance, and disease.

10 The Ignorant love food which is stale, not nourishing, putrid, and corrupt, the leavings of others and unclean.

11 Sacrifice is Pure when it is offered by one who does not covet the fruit thereof, when it is done according to the commands of scripture, and with implicit faith that the sacrifice is a duty.

12 Sacrifice which is performed for the sake of its results, or for self-glorification—that, O best of Aryans! is the product of Passion.

13 Sacrifice that is contrary to scriptural command, that is unaccompanied by prayers or gifts of food or money, and is without faith—that is the product of Ignorance.

14 Worship of God and the Master;[3] respect for the preacher and the philosopher; purity, rectitude,[4] continence,[5] and harmlessness—all this is physical austerity.

15 Speech that hurts no one, that is true,[6] is pleasant to listen to and beneficial, and the constant study of the scriptures[7]—this is austerity in speech.

16 Serenity, kindness, silence,[8] self-control, and purity—this is austerity of mind.

17 These threefold austerities performed with faith and without thought of reward, may truly be accounted Pure.

18 Austerity coupled with hypocrisy or performed for the sake of self-glorification, popularity, or vanity comes from Passion, and its result is always doubtful and temporary.

19 Austerity done under delusion, and accompanied with sorcery or torture to oneself or another, may be assumed to spring from Ignorance.

9 "Give as the rose gives perfume—because it is its own nature—utterly unconscious of giving" (Vivekananda).

10 OM TAT SAT: "The power of creation that lies in the Creator emanates from this Mantra" (Sivananda). "This name isn't just a threefold symbol; it is God Himself, so know that whatever action you may undertake, whether it is a sacrifice, a gift, or some severe penance, it may remain defective or incomplete; but if it is offered to God, it is transformed into His nature" (Jnanadeva).

In chapter 17 Krishna advises people who worship with faith but without following the scriptures to cultivate pure *sattva* in their eating habits, worship, giving, and spiritual practices. If there is any defect in their practices, repeating or remembering the name of God will have a purifying effect.

11 Verses 23–27 are "a reminder that our work should be made an expression of the triple Divine in our inner being" (Aurobindo). This may take the form of remembrance or repetition of the name of God, for "the name and the named are inseparable" (Jnanadeva).

12 OM: see ch. 7, n. 7. "The repetition of the sacred *Om* at the beginning of all actions is like an unfailing light in the darkness, or a strong companion in a forest." (Jnanadeva).

13 TAT, a reference to the Absolute, recalls the famous saying from the *Chandogya Upanishad*: *Tat tvam asi*, "Thou art That," meaning that you, like everyone else, are one with God. "So with the repetition of *Tat*, referring to the Supreme, they offer all their actions to Him. Saying, This is not mine, they cleanse themselves from the taint of action" (Jnanadeva).

14 "The word *Sat* refers to that perfect nature of reality, by which all unreality loses its value, like a counterfeit coin.... Just as a divine medicine can cure a patient, and help can be given to one who is overwhelmed, in the same way the word *Sat* can restore perfection to an action which was carried out imperfectly" (Jnanadeva).

20 The gift which is given without thought of recompense, in the belief that it ought to be made, in a fit place, at an opportune time, and to a deserving person—such a gift is Pure.[9]

21 That which is given for the sake of the results it will produce, or with the hope of recompense, or grudgingly—that may truly be said to be the outcome of Passion.

22 And that which is given at an unsuitable place or time or to one who is unworthy, or with disrespect or contempt—such a gift is the result of Ignorance.

23 OM TAT SAT[10] is the triple designation of the Eternal Spirit, by which of old the Vedic scriptures, the ceremonials, and the sacrifices were ordained.[11]

24 Therefore all acts of sacrifice, gifts, and austerities, prescribed by the scriptures, are always begun by those who understand the Spirit with the word OM.[12]

25 Those who desire deliverance begin their acts of sacrifice, austerity, or gift with the word TAT[13] (meaning "That"), without thought of reward.

26 SAT[14] means Reality or the highest Good, and also, O Arjuna! it is used to mean an action of exceptional merit.

27 Conviction in sacrifice, in austerity, and in giving is also called SAT. So too an action done only for the Lord's sake.

28 Whatsoever is done without faith, whether it be sacrifice, austerity, or gift or anything else, is called *asat* (meaning "unreal")—for it is the negation of SAT, O Arjuna! Such an act has no significance, here or hereafter.

1 Renunciation is *samnyasa*. Relinquishing is *tyaga* (abandonment), which means internal renunciation and does not imply nonaction. In India especially, people commonly understand *tyaga* to mean giving up worldly possessions and obligations, whereas "the Gita takes absolutely the opposite view that the real Tyaga has action and living in the world as its basis and not a flight to the monastery, the cave or the hill-top. The real Tyaga is action with a renunciation of desire, and that too is the real Sannyasa" (Aurobindo).

2 "Obligatory actions" include the rites, rituals, and other acts of worship (such as service or penitence) commanded by scripture, but these ought not to be performed mechanically or regarded as ends in themselves. "For most persons, spiritual *sadhana,* or practice, consists in the external observance of rituals and ceremonies prescribed by their own religion. In the initial stages such observance has its own value as a factor contributing toward self-purification and mental discipline. But ultimately the aspirant has to transcend the phase of external conformity and become initiated into the deeper aspects of spiritual *sadhana.* When this happens, the external aspect of religion falls into the background; and the aspirant gets interested in the essentials revealed in all the great religions" (Meher Baba).

18 □ The Spirit of Renunciation

Arjuna asked:

1 O Mighty One! I desire to know how relinquishing is distinguished from renunciation.

Lord Shri Krishna replied:

2 The sages say that renunciation means forgoing an action which springs from desire; and relinquishing means the surrender of its fruit.[1]

3 Some philosophers say that all action is evil and should be abandoned. Others that acts of sacrifice, benevolence, and austerity should not be given up.

4 O best of Indians! Listen to My judgment as regards this problem. It has a threefold aspect.

5 Acts of sacrifice, benevolence, and austerity should not be given up, but should be performed; for they purify the aspiring soul.

6 But they should be done with detachment, and without thought of recompense. This is My final judgment.

7 It is not right to give up actions which are obligatory;[2] and if they are misunderstood and ignored, it is the result of sheer Ignorance.

8 To avoid an action through fear of physical suffering, because it is likely to be painful, is to act from Passion, and the benefit of renunciation will not follow.

9 He who performs an obligatory action, because he believes it to be a duty which ought to be done, without any personal desire either to do

3 | Philosophy: literally, the Samkhya doctrine.

4 | Personality: *kartri*, agent of action, doer. "The doer is ordinarily sup-
posed to be our surface personal ego, but that is the false idea of the
understanding that has not arrived at knowledge. The ego is the osten-
sible doer, but the ego and its will are the creations and instruments of
Nature, with which the ignorant understanding wrongly identifies our
self, and they are not the only determinants" (Aurobindo).

the act or to receive any return—such renunciation is Pure.

10 The wise man who has attained purity, whose doubts are solved, who is filled with the spirit of self-abnegation, does not shrink from action because it brings pain, nor does he desire it because it brings pleasure.

11 But since those still in the body cannot entirely avoid action, in their case abandonment of the fruit of action is considered as complete renunciation.

12 For those who cannot renounce all desire, the fruit of action hereafter is threefold—good, evil, and partly good and partly evil. But for him who has renounced, there is none.

13 I will tell you now, O Mighty Man! the five causes which, according to the final decision of philosophy,[3] must concur before an action can be accomplished.

14 They are a body, a personality,[4] physical organs, their manifold activity, and destiny.

15 Whatever action a man perform, whether by muscular effort or by speech or by thought, and whether it be right or wrong, these five are the essential causes.

16 But the fool who supposes, because of his immature judgment, that it is his own Self alone that acts, he perverts the truth, and does not see rightly.

17 He who has no pride, and whose intellect is unalloyed by attachment, even though he kill these people, yet he does not kill them, and his act does not bind him.

18 Knowledge, the knower, and the object of knowledge, these are the threefold incentives to action; and the act, the actor, and the instrument are the threefold constituents.

19 The knowledge, the act, and the doer differ according to the Qualities.

@ "The essence of the Gita is what you get by repeating the word ten times. The word becomes reversed. It is then *tagi*, which refers to renunciation. The essence of the Gita is: O man, renounce everything and practice spiritual discipline for the realization of God."

—Ramakrishna

Listen to this too:

20 That knowledge which sees the One Indestructible in all beings, the One Indivisible in all separate lives, may be truly called Pure Knowledge.

21 The knowledge which thinks of the manifold existence in all beings as separate—that comes from Passion.

22 But that which clings blindly to one idea as if it were all, without logic, truth, or insight, that has its origin in Darkness.

23 An obligatory action done by one who is disinterested, who neither likes it nor dislikes it, and gives no thought to the consequences that follow, such an action is Pure.

24 But even though an action involve the most strenuous endeavor, yet if the doer is seeking to gratify his desires and is filled with personal vanity, it may be assumed to originate in Passion.

25 An action undertaken through delusion, and with no regard to the spiritual issues involved, or to the real capacity of the doer, or to the injury which may follow, such an act may be assumed to be the product of Ignorance.

26 But when a man has no sentiment and no personal vanity, when he possesses courage and confidence, cares not whether he succeeds or fails, then his action arises from Purity.

27 In him who is impulsive, greedy, looking for reward, violent, impure, torn between joy and sorrow, it may be assumed that in him Passion is predominant.

28 While he whose purpose is infirm, who is low-minded, stubborn, dishonest, malicious, indolent, despondent, procrastinating—he may be assumed to be in Darkness.

29 Reason and conviction are threefold, according to the Quality which is

⟐ "The English word 'renounce' strikes a cold note, but the Sanskrit word *tyaga* implies a positive, joyful act in which we find fulfillment. In the words of Jesus, we have to lose ourselves to find ourselves."

—Eknath Easwaran

dominant. I will explain them fully and severally, O Arjuna!

30 That intellect which understands the creation and dissolution of life, what actions should be done and what not, which discriminates between fear and fearlessness, bondage and deliverance, that is Pure.

31 The intellect which does not understand what is right and what is wrong, and what should be done and what not, is under the sway of Passion.

32 And that which, shrouded in Ignorance, thinks wrong right, and sees everything perversely, O Arjuna! that intellect is ruled by Darkness.

33 The conviction and steady concentration by which the mind, the vitality, and the senses are controlled—O Arjuna! they are the product of Purity.

34 The conviction which always holds fast to rituals, to self-interest and wealth, for the sake of what they may bring forth—that comes from Passion.

35 And that which clings perversely to false idealism, fear, grief, despair, and vanity—it is the product of Ignorance.

36 Hear further the three kinds of pleasure. That which increases day after day and delivers one from misery,

37 Which at first seems like poison but afterward acts like nectar—that pleasure is Pure, for it is born of Wisdom.

38 That which at first is like nectar, because the senses revel in their objects, but in the end acts like poison—that pleasure arises from Passion.

39 While the pleasure which from first to last merely drugs the senses, which springs from indolence, lethargy, and folly—that pleasure flows from Ignorance.

5 This verse concerns the four social divisions (*varnas*) of ancient India: brahmins (priests and educators), kshatriyas (warriors and rulers), vaishyas (producers and merchants), and shudras (servants and laborers). The word *varna* is usually translated "caste" but should be distinguished from the degraded concept of caste *(jati)* in contemporary Indian society. *Varna* literally means "color," which some commentators interpret in an esoteric manner, as referring not to skin color but to the aura, a subtle energy field around a person (perceptible to some as colored light) that reflects the nature of his or her mental impressions. The four *varnas* were thus originally based on innate qualities and outward actions of people. According to Yogananda, the shudra is identified with body consciousness and the senses; the vaishya cultivates wisdom; the kshatriya practices self-control to protect his or her mental kingdom from invasion by ego forces; and the brahmin possesses knowledge of Spirit. "In order to be a brahmin, we do not need to wear a sacred thread or to undergo purification ceremonies. Whoever tries to know Brahman, the supreme Reality embedded within him, is a brahmin" (Easwaran). The Buddha expresses a similar view in *Dhammapada* 26 ("The Brahmin").

Sri Aurobindo says that each of us has all four "castes" in our spiritual nature—"a soul of knowledge, a soul of strength and of power, a soul of mutuality and interchange, a soul of works and service." Usually one of these predominates in an individual and colors his or her expression of the other three. In life we follow our predominant nature "not crudely and rigidly" (as in the caste system) but "subtly and flexibly." By developing our own essential nature and being true to ourselves, we develop the other three powers as well. Thus, says Sri Aurobindo, if we follow a natural impulse to service (the "servant" within us) "rightly done"—that is, if we help others without self-interest or attachment to results—we will simultaneously develop our knowledge (the spiritual teacher), increase our power (the soldier), and cultivate the art of relationship (the trader).

"The quality of a person can be neither determined nor circumscribed by any man-made birth-caste classification" (Yogananda).

40 There is nothing anywhere on earth or in the higher worlds which is free from the three Qualities—for they are born of Nature.

41 O Arjuna! The duties of the spiritual teachers, the soldiers, the traders, and the servants have all been fixed according to the dominant Quality in their nature.[5]

42 Serenity, self-restraint, austerity, purity, forgiveness, as well as uprightness, knowledge, wisdom, and faith in God—these constitute the duty of a spiritual Teacher.

43 Valor, glory, firmness, skill, generosity, steadiness in battle, and ability to rule—these constitute the duty of a soldier. They flow from his own nature.

44 Agriculture, protection of the cow, and trade are the duty of a trader; again in accordance with his nature. The duty of a servant is to serve, and that too agrees with his nature.

45 Perfection is attained when each attends diligently to his duty. Listen and I will tell you how it is attained by him who always minds his own duty.

46 Man reaches perfection by dedicating his actions to God, Who is the source of all being, and fills everything.

47 It is better to do one's own duty, however defective it may be, than to follow the duty of another, however well one may perform it. He who does his duty as his own nature reveals it, never sins.

48 The duty that of itself falls to one's lot should not be abandoned, though it may have its defects. All acts are marred by defects, as fire is obscured by smoke.

49 He whose mind is entirely detached, who has conquered himself, whose desires have vanished, by his renunciation, reaches that stage of perfect freedom where action completes itself and leaves no seed.

6 By such devotion, he sees Me: Prabhavananda and Isherwood translate this line simply as: "To love is to know me."

@ "Chaitanya (1486–1533), the ecstatic founder of Bengal Vaishnavism, once came upon a man reading the Bhagavadgita aloud in a temple, and as he read everyone laughed at him, for he mispronounced all of the words. The man himself was weeping and trembling, and Chaitanya asked him which words made him cry so. 'I don't know the meaning of any of the words,' the man confessed, 'but as I sound them out I see Krishna in Arjuna's chariot. He is holding the reins in his hands and he is speaking to Arjuna and he looks very beautiful. The vision makes me weep with joy.' Chaitanya smiled: 'You are an authority on the Bhagavadgita. You know the real meaning of the text.'"

—*Encyclopedia of Religion*

50 I will now state briefly how he who has reached perfection finds the Eternal Spirit, the state of Supreme Wisdom.

51 Guided always by pure reason, bravely restraining himself, renouncing the objects of sense, and giving up attachment and hatred;

52 Enjoying solitude, abstemious, his body, mind, and speech under perfect control, absorbed in meditation, he becomes free—always filled with the spirit of renunciation.

53 Having abandoned selfishness, power, arrogance, anger, and desire, possessing nothing of his own, and having attained peace, he is fit to join the Eternal Spirit.

54 And when he becomes one with the Eternal, and his soul knows the bliss that belongs to the Self, he feels no desire and no regret, he regards all beings equally, and enjoys the blessing of supreme devotion to Me.

55 By such devotion, he sees Me,[6] who I am and what I am; and thus realizing the Truth, he enters My Kingdom.

56 Relying on Me in all his actions and doing them for My sake, he attains, by My grace, Eternal and Unchangeable Life.

57 Surrender then your actions unto Me, live in Me, concentrate your intellect on Me, and think always of Me.

58 Fix but your mind on Me, and by My grace you shall overcome the obstacles in your path. But if, misled by pride, you will not listen, then indeed you shall be lost.

59 If you in your vanity think of avoiding this fight, your will shall not be fulfilled, for Nature herself will compel you.

60 O Arjuna! Your duty binds you. From your own nature has it arisen, and that which in your delusion you desire not to do, that very thing you shall do. You are helpless.

7 Wheel: *yantra*, mechanism, machine. Mystic power: Maya. An alternative translation is "...making them all revolve like puppets on a carousel" (Mitchell). "From behind the veil of cosmic illusion, He holds the string with which He causes countless numbers of species to dance like shadow pictures on a screen" (Jnanadeva). All beings are like toys in God's divine game, which he inspires with his life-giving love (Meher Baba). "We are all being dragged along by this mighty, complex world-machine. There are only two ways out of it. One is to give up all concern with the machine and stand aside—that is, to give up all desires. That is very easy to say, but almost impossible to do. The other way is to plunge into the world and learn the secret of work, and that is the way of karma-yoga. Do not fly away from the wheels of the world-machine, but stand inside it and learn the secret of work. Through proper work done inside, it is always possible to come out. Through this machine itself is the way out" (Vivekananda).

8 Up until now, Krishna has been emphasizing the importance of doing one's duty according to the principles of *karma yoga*. Now, however, the Gita reveals that it is possible to dispense with such disciplines and follow a direct path to God through love, obedience, and surrender to the Avatar. In Sri Aurobindo's paraphrase: "All this personal effort and self-discipline will not in the end be needed, all following and limitation of rule and Dharma can at last be thrown away as hampering encumbrances, if thou canst make a complete surrender to Me.... I repeat the absolute assurance, the infallible promise that I will lead thee to Myself through and beyond all sorrow and evil."

What does "surrender" imply? Yogananda suggests some meanings of this line: "Always keep your consciousness in My sheltering Presence"; "Remember Me alone"; and "Withdraw into the shelter of oneness with Me."

61 God dwells in the hearts of all beings, O Arjuna! He causes them to revolve as it were on a wheel by His mystic power.[7]

62 With all your strength, fly unto Him, and surrender yourself, and by His grace shall you attain Supreme Peace and reach the Eternal Home.

63 Thus have I revealed to you the Truth, the Mystery of mysteries. Having thought over it, you are free to act as you will.

64 Only listen once more to My last word, the deepest secret of all; you are My beloved, you are My friend, and I speak for your welfare.

65 Dedicate yourself to Me, worship Me, sacrifice all for Me, prostrate yourself before Me, and to Me you shall surely come. Truly do I pledge to you; you are My own beloved.

66 Give up then your earthly duties, surrender yourself to Me only. Do not be anxious; I will absolve you from all your sin.[8]

67 Speak not this to one who has not practiced austerities, or to him who does not love, or who will not listen, or who mocks.

68 But he who teaches this great secret to My devotees, his is the highest devotion, and verily he shall come unto Me.

69 Nor is there among men any who can perform a service dearer to Me than this, or any man on earth more beloved by Me than he.

70 He who will study this spiritual discourse of ours, I assure you, he shall thereby worship Me at the altar of Wisdom.

71 Yea, he who listens to it with faith, and without doubt, even he, freed from evil, shall rise to the worlds which the virtuous attain through righteous deeds.

72 O Arjuna! Have you listened attentively to My words? Have your ignorance and your delusion gone?

📧 Meher Baba said: "Everything in the Gita is expressed in these few lines by the Western mystic":

Take my life, and let it be consecrated, Lord, to Thee.
Take my moments and my days; let them flow in ceaseless praise.
Take my hands, and let them move at the impulse of Thy love.
Take my feet, and let them be swift and beautiful for Thee.
Take my voice, and let me sing always, only, for my King.
Take my lips, and let them be filled with messages from Thee.
Take my silver and my gold; not a mite would I withhold.
Take my intellect, and use every power as Thou shalt choose.
Take my will, and make it Thine; it shall be no longer mine.
Take my heart, it is Thine own; it shall be Thy royal throne.
Take my love, my Lord, I pour at Thy feet its treasure store.
Take myself, and I will be ever, only, all for Thee.

—hymn by Francis Ridley Havergal (1874)

Arjuna replied:

73 My Lord! O Immutable One! My delusion has fled. By Your Grace, O Changeless One, the light has dawned. My doubts are gone, and I stand before You ready to do Your will.

Sanjaya told:

74 Thus have I heard this rare, wonderful, and soul-stirring discourse of the Lord Shri Krishna and the great-souled Arjuna.

75 Through the blessing of the sage Vyasa, I listened to this secret and noble science from the lips of its Master, the Lord Shri Krishna.

76 King! The more I think of that marvelous and holy discourse, the more I lose myself in joy.

77 As memory recalls again and again the exceeding beauty of the Lord, I am filled with amazement and happiness.

78 Wherever is the Lord Shri Krishna, the Prince of Wisdom, and wherever is Arjuna, the Great Archer, I am more than convinced that good fortune, victory, happiness, and righteousness will follow.

May the Lord Shri Krishna bless you!

☐ Notes

Epigraph, p. v ("You are the greatest book..."): Vivekananda, *Living at the Source: Yoga Teachings of Vivekananda*, edited by Ann Myren and Dorothy Madison (Boston : Shambhala Publications, 1993), 35.

"About the *Bhagavad Gita*": Vivekananda (on "the best authority on Vedanta"), *The Yogas and Other Works*, 544. Aurobindo (on extracting the living truths), *Essays on the Gita*, 1:6–7. Eliot Deutsch and Lee Siegel, "Bhagavadgita," *Encyclopedia of Religion*, 2:128. Aurobindo ("though he is manifest..."), *Essays*, 1:255–56. Nikhilananda, *Bhagavad Gita*, 30. Aurobindo (on historicity of Krishna), *Essays*, 1:21.

Chapter 1

1. Chinmoy, *Commentary on the Bhagavad Gita*, 1. Miller, *The Bhagavad-Gita*, 165.

6. Yogananda, *God Talks with Arjuna*, 111–114.

7. *Katha Upanishad* (1.3), Purohit & Yeats, *Ten Principal Upanishads*, 32.

"Just as the first day...": Sargeant, 27.

10. Maharishi, *Bhagavad Gita*, 47.

11. Aurobindo, *Dictionary*, 270.

14. Nikhilananda, 66.

"All life is a battlefield...": Easwaran, *The End of Sorrow*, 43.

Chapter 2

1. Feuerstein, *Shambhala Encyclopedia of Yoga*, 33. On the "Aryan invasion" theory, see Georg Feuerstein, Subhash Kak, and David Frawley, *In Search of the Cradle of Civilization* (Wheaton, Ill.: Quest Books, 1995).

2. Gandhi, M. K. *Gandhi Interprets the Bhagvadgita*, 14.

3. On Bhishma's bed of arrows, see Walter O. Kaelber, "Asceticism," *Encyclopedia of Religion*, 1: 443.

5. Maharishi, 89, Yogananda, 194.

6. Meher Baba, quoted in Bhau Kalchuri, *Lord Meher*, vol. 7 (Myrtle Beach, S.C.: Manifestation, Inc., 1994), 2452.

7. Nikhilananda, 73.

8. Yogananda, 206.

10. Gandhi, 32.

"The Gita is not a justification...": Thomas Merton, "The Significance of the *Bhagavad Gita*," in Bhaktivedanta, *Bhagavad Gita As It Is* (1968), 20.

"The various schools...": Chinmoy, *Commentary on the Bhagavad Gita*, 18.

18. Maharishi, 132.

19. Feuerstein, *Shambhala Encyclopedia of Yoga*, 67.

22. Easwaran, *The End of Sorrow*, 103–4.

23. *Gospel of Sri Ramakrishna*, 181.

24. Mircea Eliade, "Yoga," *Encyclopedia of Religion*, 15:521. Maharishi, *Bhagavad Gita*, 158.

27. David Frawley, *Ayurveda and the Mind: The Healing of Consciousness* (Twin Lakes, Wisc.: Lotus Press, 1996), 93–94.

28. Bhaktivedanta, *Bhagavad Gita As It Is* (1972), online at www.asitis.com.

32. Easwaran, *The End of Sorrow*, 212.

"One of the beauties....": Easwaran, *The End of Sorrow*, 92.

Chapter 3

1. Meher Baba, *Discourses*, 253–54.

2. Aurobindo, *Dictionary*, 222.

"Let us give up...": Vivekananda, *The Yogas and Other Works*, 499.

"There are two types of ego": Meher Baba, quoted in Bill Le Page, *The Turning of the Key: Meher Baba in Australia* (Myrtle Beach, S.C.: Sheriar Press, 1993), 62.

7. Yogananda, 394.

9. Meher Baba, *Discourses*, 331.

10. Maharishi, 233.

"Any action...": Vivekananda, *Living at the Source: Yoga Teachings of Vivekananda*, edited by Ann Myren and Dorothy Madison (Boston : Shambhala Publications, 1993), 68.

13. Shankara, *Bhagavad Gita*, 117.

Chapter 4

2. Yogananda, 424.

5. Nikhilananda, 126.

8. Easwaran, *The End of Sorrow*, 230.

12. Aurobindo, *Gita*, 66.

18. Easwaran, *The End of Sorrow,* 277.
19. Arthur Osborne, *The Incredible Sai Baba.* New York: Samuel Weiser, 1972), 23; Antonio Rigopoulos, *The Life and Teachings of Sai Baba of Shirdi* (Albany: SUNY Press, 1993), 130.

"As the sharp edge...": Maharishi, 322.

Chapter 5

6. Ramanuja, 196. Edgerton, 94.
12. Edgerton, 185. Meher Baba, *Discourses,* 91.
13. Nikhilananda, 159. Meher Baba, *Discourses,* 190.
15. Ramanuja, 210.

Chapter 6

1. Besant, 79. Shankhara, 184. Swami Swarupananda, quoted by Nikhilananda, 161.
2. Yogananda, 599.
3. Gandhi, 165. *Gospel of Sri Ramakrishna,* 476.
4. Yogananda, 600.
5. Ramanuja, *Sri Ramanuja Gita Bhasya,* 218. Maharishi, 404.
6. Yogananda, 604.
8. Yogananda, 608. Aurobindo, *Gita,* 84. Maharishi, 408. Shankara, 191.
9. Maharishi, 410.
13. Edgerton, 185. Demetrios J. Constantelos, "Charity," *Encyclopedia of Religion,* 3:224.
14. Prabhavananda, *Narada's Way of Divine Love,* 40. Feuerstein, *Shambhala Encyclopedia of Yoga,* 319.

"When a man of the world...": Huston Smith, *The Illustrated World Religions* (San Francisco: HarperSanFrancisco, 1994), 21.

15. Meher Baba, *God to Man and Man to God: The Discourses of Meher Baba,* edited by C. B. Purdom (North Myrtle Beach, S.C.: Sheriar Press, 1975), 32.
16. Edgerton, 168–69.

Chapter 7

1. Vivekananda, *The Yogas and Other Works,* 321. Gandhi, 182.
5. Nikhilananda, 181.
7. Meher Baba, *Beams from Meher Baba on the Spiritual Panorama* (Walnut Creek, Calif.: Sufism Reoriented, 1958), 19. Yogananda, 1007.

9. Meher Baba, quoted in Manija Sheriar Irani, *Eighty-two Family Letters* (North Myrtle Beach, S.C.: Sheriar Press, 1976), 265.

10. Nikhilananda, 186.

11. Yogananda, 949. Ramanuja, 253. Jnanadeva, *Jnaneshwar's Gita*, 238. Nikhilananda, 218. Ramana Maharshi, quoted in Ken Wilber, *Eye to Eye* (Boston: Shambhala, 2001), 140. The saying by Shankara occurs in verse 20 of his *Viveka-chudamani* ("Crest Jewel of Discrimination").

12. Diana L. Eck, *Darśan: Seeing the Divine in India* (Chambersburg, Pa.: Anima Books, 1985), 3. On meditating on the image of perfection, see Meher Baba, *Discourses*, 230–32. Yogananda, 699.

"Age after age...": Meher Baba, *Listen, Humanity,* 227.

Chapter 8

7. Feuerstein, *Shambhala Encyclopedia of Yoga*, 223.

9. Yogananda, 738–39.

10. Nikhilananda, 211. Bhaktivedanta, *Bhagavad Gita As It Is,* www.asitis.com.

12. Aurobindo, *Gita*, 111.

Chapter 9

4. Bhaktivedanta, www.asitis.com. Meher Baba, *Discourses*, 269.

5. Sivananda, *Bhagavad Gita* (online). *Gospel of Sri Ramakrishna*, 150.

6. Feuerstein, *Shambhala Encyclopedia of Yoga,* 21.

8. Prabhavananda, *Narada's Way of Divine Love*, 112–13.

9. Gandhi, 210.

10. Easwaran, *Like a Thousand Suns,* 183. Prabhavananda, *Narada's Way of Divine Love*, 54.

12. Ramanuja, 322. *Devi-Bhagavata*, quoted by Vivekananda, *Yogas and Other Works*, 444.

13. Meher Baba, *Listen, Humanity*, narrated and edited by D. E. Stevens (New York: Harper & Row, 1971), 17.

Chapter 10

2. Gandhi, quoted in Yogananda, 961.

4. Edgerton, 97. Purohit Swami, *Geeta*, 58.

5. Prabhavananda, *Narada's Way of Divine Love*, 55–56.

8. Meher Baba, *Discourses*, 141.

9. Aurobindo, *Essays*, 2:160. Meher Baba, *Discourses*, 63.

12. Aurobindo, *Gita*, 132. Feuerstein, *Shambhala Encyclopedia of Yoga,* 129.

19. Yogananda, 792.
24. Ramanuja, 349.
26. Bhaktivedanta, www.asitis.com.
28. Yogananda, 808.
30. Vivekananda, *The Yogas and Other Works*, 739. Edgerton, 128.

Chapter 11

"In this climactic chapter...": Mitchell, 29. Rudolf Otto, *Das Heilige* (1917), translated as *The Idea of the Holy* (1923).
1. Bhaktivedanta, www.asitis.com, commentary on 11.8.
3. Yogananda, 821.
5. Feuerstein, *Shambhala Encyclopedia of Yoga*, 26.
11. Aurobindo, *Essays*, 2:185.
12. Yogananda, 1030.
"Krishna, as the Avatar...": Meher Baba, *Discourses*, 80–81.
"The Self is universal...": *The Spiritual Teaching of Ramana Maharshi* (Boston: Shambhala Publications, 1988), 43.
13. Shankara, 294.
15. Aurobindo, *Essays*, 2:192.
16. Aurobindo, *Dictionary*, 31.
17. Edgerton, 178.

Chapter 12

"An intense search...": Shankara, quoted in Vivekananda, *Yogas and Other Works*, 544.
1. Edgerton, 167. Meher Baba, *Discourses*, 264, 8, 262.
"When love is deep...": Meher Baba, *Discourses*, 55–56.
2. Jnanadeva, *Jnaneshwar's Gita*, 178.
3. Nikhilananda, 277.
4. Jnanadeva, 181.
5. Sargeant, 522.
6. Sivananda, *Bhagavad Gita* (online).
7. Shastri, *Narada Sutras*, 62.
8. Aurobindo, *Essays*, 2 :172.
"A true devotee...": Prabhavananda, *Narada's Way of Divine Love*, 17.
"Anyone who has perceived...": Pai and Mulick, *The Gita*, 21.

Chapter 13

1. Nikhilananda, 283.
2. Shankara, 337.
3. Jnanadeva, 209.
4. Ramanuja, 445.
5. Aurobindo, *Gita*, 173.
6. Georg Feuerstein, "Yoga and Meditation (Dhyana)," *Moksha Journal*, Winter 1996/97. Published by Yoga Anand Ashram, Amityville, N.Y. Online edition at www.santosha.com.

"Nature's task...": Vivekananda, *Living at the Source*, 124–25.

Chapter 14

Parable of Ramakrishna: *The Encyclopedia of Eastern Philosophy and Religion* (Boston: Shambhala Publications, 1989), 121. *Gospel of Sri Ramakrishna*, 268.

2. Easwaran, *The End of Sorrow*, 237–38.
3. Jnanadeva, 230.
4. Jnanadeva, 231.
5. Edgerton, 170.

"Neither seek nor avoid...": Vivekananda, *Yogas and Other Works*, 517.

6. Jnanadeva, 233.

Chapter 15

2. *Gospel of Sri Ramakrishna*, 103. Jnanadeva, 245.
3. Shankara, 402–3.
5. Yogananda, 943–44.
7. Jnanadeva, 253–54.

Chapter 16

2. Ramanuja, 506. Meher Baba, *Listen, Humanity*, 183.
3. Gandhi, 256.
4. Meher Baba, quoted in Bhau Kalchuri, *Lord Meher*, vol. 7 (Myrtle Beach, S.C.: Manifestation, 1994), 2359. Yogananda, 963.
6. Aurobindo, *Essays*, 2:318.

"It must not be thought...": Nikhilananda, 189–90.

7. Meher Baba, *Discourses*, 11. Yogananda, 978.
8. Meher Baba, *Listen, Humanity*, 44.
9. Gandhi, 260. Aurobindo, *Gita*, 203.

"Do you know the use...": *Gospel of Sri Ramakrishna*, 882–83.

Chapter 17

"'Faith' here is not....": Easwaran, *To Love Is to Know Me*, 305.

2. Frawley, *Ayurveda and the Mind: The Healing of Consciousness* (Twin Lakes, Wisc.: Lotus Press, 1996), 192–93.
3. Prabhavananda & Isherwood, 118. Yogananda, 1000.
6. Yogananda, 961. Meher Baba, quoted in Eruch Jessawala, *That's How It Was* (Myrtle Beach, S.C.: Sheriar Foundation, 1995), 180.
7. Feuerstein, *Shambhala Encyclopedia of Yoga*, 299. Yogananda, 1000.
8. Feuerstein, "Yoga and Meditation (Dhyana)." Yogananda, 1001. Nikhilananda, 339.
9. Vivekananda, *Living at the Source: Yoga Teachings of Vivekananda*, edited by Ann Myren and Dorothy Madison (Boston: Shambhala Publications, 1993), 100.
10. Sivananda, *Bhagavad Gita* (online). Jnanadeva, 287.
11. Aurobindo, *Gita*, 211. Jnanadeva, 287.
12. Jnanadeva, 286.
13. Jnanadeva, 287.
14. Ibid.

Chapter 18

1. Aurobindo, *Gita*, 215.
"The essence of the Gita....": *Gospel of Sri Ramakrishna*, 255.
"The English word 'renounce'....": Easwaran, *The End of Sorrow*, 293.
1. Meher Baba, *Discourses*, 258.
4. Aurobindo, *Gita*, 217.
5. Yogananda, 1065. Easwaran, *The End of Sorrow*, 165. Aurobindo, *Gita*, 224–25. "The quality of a person..." Yogananda, 1064.
6. Prabhavanada & Isherwood, 128.
Chaitanya story: Eliot Deutsch and Lee Siegel, "Bhagavadgita," *Encyclopedia of Religion*, 2:128.
7. Jnanadeva, 334. Meher Baba, *Everything & Nothing* (Sydney: Meher House Publications, 1963), 71. Vivekananda, *The Yogas and Other Works*, 507.
8. Aurobindo, *Gita*, 232–33. Yogananda, 1089.
Meher Baba on the Havergal hymn: *Treasures from the Meher Baba Journals*, 1938–1942, compiled and edited by Jane Barry Haynes (Myrtle Beach, S.C.: Sheriar Press, 1980), 62–63.

Suggested Readings and Resources □

Translations and Commentaries

Aurobindo, Sri (1872–1950). *Essays on the Gita.* 2 vols. Calcutta: Arya Publishing House, 1928. Profound and brilliant writings by one of the great spiritual leaders of our times.

————. *The Gita.* With text, translation, and Sri Aurobindo's comments. Edited by Shyam Sunder Jhunjhunwala. Auroville: Auropublications, 1974. Commentary excerpted from the *Essays on the Gita.*

Besant, Annie (1847–1933). *The Bhagavad Gita: The Lord's Song* (1895). Madras: Theosophical Publishing House, 2003. First ed., 1895. A respectable translation with brief notes and index, by the noted Theosophist.

Bhaktivedanta Swami Prabhupada, A. C. (1896–1977). *The Bhagavad Gita as It Is: A New Translation, with Commentary.* New York: Macmillan, 2008. The searchable (1972) text is online at www.asitis.com. Srila Prabhupada (as he is now called) was the founder of the International Society for Krishna Consciousness (the "Hare Krishna" movement). "Krishna consciousness" means a pure state of consciousness in harmony with Krishna.

Chinmoy, Sri (born 1931). *Commentary on the Bhagavad Gita: The Song of the Transcendental Soul.* Blauvelt, N.Y.: Rudolf Steiner Publications, 1973. General, inspirational comments, without accompanying translation. Sri Chinmoy is a teacher of meditation as well as an artist, musician, and advocate for world peace.

Easwaran, Eknath (1911–1999). *The Bhagavad Gita for Daily Living,* 3 vols. Vol. 1 (chaps. 1–6), *The End of Sorrow.* Vol. 2 (chaps. 7–12), *Like a Thousand Suns.* Vol. 3 (chaps. 8–18), *To Love Is to Know Me.* Tomales, Calif.: Nilgiri Press, 1979. A popular and respected meditation teacher, Sri Easwaran was the author of twenty-four books. His free translation of the Gita is heartfelt and accessible, allowing a broad interpretation. His engaging commentary is focused on putting the Gita into practice in everyday life. An edition of his translation of the Gita without the extensive commentary is also available. See www.easwaran.org.

Edgerton, Franklin (1885–1963). *The Bhagavad Gita.* Cambridge: Harvard University Press, 1997. First ed., 1925. Literal translation and scholarly interpretation by a respected professor.

Gandhi, Mahatma (1869–1948). *M. K. Gandhi Interprets the Bhagvadgita.* Ahmedabad: Navajivan Trust, n.d. The great political leader, pacifist, and social reformer was a devoted student of the Gita. This work is based on discourses given in 1926.

Jnanadeva (13th century). *Jnaneshwar's Gita: A Rendering of the Jnaneshwari,* by Swami Kripananda. South Fallsburg, N.Y.: SYDA Foundation, 1999. This wonderful, divinely inspired commentary is a classic of Marathi literature (written in the language of the Indian state of Maharashtra). Jnanadeva (also known as Jnaneshwar), a leader of the *bhakti* or devotional tradition, became fully realized while still in his teens. This is the best English version available.

Maharishi Mahesh Yogi (born 1920?). *Bhagavad-Gita: A New Translation and Commentary, Chapters 1–6.* New York: Penguin Books, 1979. Insightful commentary by the founder of the Transcendental Meditation movement. Unfortunately, Maharishi has not published his commentary on chapters 7–18.

Mascaró, Juan. *The Bhagavad Gita.* London: Penguin Books, 2010. A translation appreciated by many for its literary quality.

Merton, Thomas. "The Significance of the *Bhagavad Gita,*" in A. C. Bhaktivedanta, *The Bhagavad Gita as It Is: A New Translation, with Commentary.* New York: Collier Books, 2008.

Miller, Barbara Stoler. *The Bhagavad-Gita: Krishna's Counsel in Time of War.* New York: Bantam Books, 2004. A readable verse translation by a respected professor at Barnard College, Columbia University, who died in 1993.

Mitchell, Stephen. *Bhagavad Gita: A New Translation.* New York: Three Rivers Press, 2006. An enjoyable, well-crafted verse rendition by an accomplished poet, aimed at the contemporary reader.

Nikhilananda, Swami. *The Bhagavad Gita* (1944). Translated from the Sanskrit with notes, comments, and introduction. New York: Ramakrishna-Vivekananda Center, 1978. With interesting notes and commentary mainly following the view of Shankara. Some of the commentary is drawn from Aurobindo's writings on the Gita (but not cited).

Prabhavananda, Swami, and Christopher Isherwood. *The Song of God: Bhagavad-Gita* (1944). New York: New American Library, 1972. Part verse and part prose. Isherwood was a popular British novelist, a pacifist, an advocate of gay rights, and a devotee of Vedanta. Swami Prabhavananda, a monk in the Ramakrishna order, was his guru.

Purohit Swami, Shri (1882–1941). *The Geeta: The Gospel of Lord Shri Krishna* (1935). London: Faber and Faber, 1978.

Ramanuja, Sri (1017–1137). *Sri Ramanuja Gita Bhasya.* Translated by Svami Adidevananda. Myalpore, Madras: Sri Ramakrishna Math, 2007. Ramanuja was a Vaishnava spiritual leader (Vaishnavism is the worship of Vishnu), the foremost exponent of the "qualified nondualist" school of Vedanta, and the chief opponent of Shankara's philosophy. He taught the supremacy of the personal aspect of God (Krishna) and the importance of surrender to God.

Sargeant, Winthrop (trans.). *The Bhagavad Gita.* Albany: SUNY Press, 2009. A literal version, not very readable but useful for its word-by-word translation and inclusion of both the Devanagari script and transliteration.

Shankara (788–820 or c. 700). *The Bhagavad Gita.* With the Commentary of Sri Sankaracharya. Translated by Alladi Mahadeva Sastry. Madras: Samata Books, 2013. (First ed., 1897.) The oldest existing commentary, by the great proponent of Advaita (nondualistic) Vedanta. His teachings emphasize the absolute oneness of God, who is the only Reality; all apparent multiplicity is an illusion.

Sivananda, Swami (1887–1963). *The Bhagavad Gita.* Shivanandanagar: Divine Life Society, 2010. A modern master of yoga, founder of the Divine Life Society.

Yogananda, Paramahansa (1893–1952). *God Talks with Arjuna: The Bhagavad Gita, Royal Science of God Realization.* 2 vols. Second ed. Los Angeles: Self-Realization Fellowship, 2001. Yogananda is the author of the very popular book *Autobiography of a Yogi.* Here, in two volumes, he interprets the Gita as an allegorical exposition of the practices of yoga and includes detailed discussions of technical aspects of yoga as well as in-depth comments on symbolism in the text. He also provides interesting comments comparing the teachings of yoga with those of science and Christianity.

Audio and Video Resources

Srimad Bhagavadgita, Gandharva Music Productions, 1992. Audio series featuring Vedic pandits Ramesh Vardhan and Ram Chandra Joshi reciting the Sanskrit text (without musical accompaniment).

The Mahabharata, the 1989 film by Peter Brook, based on his translation of Jean-Claude Carrière's 9-hour stage version. The video was broadcast in a 6-hour version on public television, and it is also available in a 3-hour version. Although the Gita is only a brief episode in it, the film presents the epic context of the Gita and is notable for its multiracial cast.

Comic Book

Pai, Anant (script), and Pratap Mulick (artwork). *The Gita.* Amar Chitra Katha series, vol. 505. Mumbai: India Book House Ltd., 2007. A good summary and introduction for children and adults.

Other References

Adiswarananda, Swami (1925–2007). *The Four Yogas: A Guide to the Spiritual Paths of Action, Devotion, Meditation and Knowledge.* Woodstock, Vt.: SkyLight Paths, 2006.

———. *The Vedanta Way to Peace and Happiness.* Woodstock, Vt.: SkyLight Paths, 2004.

——— (ed.). *Vivekananda, World Teacher.* Woodstock, Vt.: SkyLight Paths, 2006.

Aurobindo, Sri. *Dictionary of Sri Aurobindo's Yoga.* Twin Lakes, Wis.: Lotus Press, 1992.

Encyclopedia of Religion. Mircea Eliade, editor. 16 vols. New York: Macmillan, 1987.

Feuerstein, Georg. *The Shambhala Encyclopedia of Yoga.* Boston: Shambhala Publications, 1997. For more of Feuerstein's writings, see his Yoga Research and Education Center website at www.yrec.org.

Harvey, Andrew. *A Walk with Four Spiritual Guides: Krishna, Buddha, Jesus, and Ramakrishna.* Woodstock, Vt.: SkyLight Paths, 2005.

Meher Baba (1894–1969). *Discourses.* Seventh rev. ed. Myrtle Beach, S.C.: Sheriar Foundation, 1987. This outstanding spiritual figure is loved and worshiped as the Avatar by people of different religions throughout the world.

Nikhilananda, Swami (1895-1973). *Selections from the Gospel of Sri Ramakrishna: Annotated & Explained.* Annotated by Kendra Crossen Burroughs. Woodstock, Vt.: SkyLight Paths, 2002.

Nikhilananda, Swami, and Dhan Gopal Mukerji. *Sri Ramakrishna, the Face of Silence.* Edited with an introduction by Swami Adiswarananda. Woodstock, Vt.: SkyLight Paths, 2005.

Prabhavananda, Swami (trans.). *Narada's Way of Divine Love.* Madras: Sri Ramakrishna Math, 1999.

Purohit Swami, Shree, and W. B. Yeats (trans.). *The Ten Principal Upanishads* (1937). New Delhi: Rupa & Co., 2005.

Ramakrishna (1836–1886). *The Gospel of Sri Ramakrishna.* Translated by Swami Nikhilananda. New York: Ramakrishna-Vivekananda Center, 2007. One of the greatest universal Masters of modern times, Ramakrishna was noted for his worship of the Divine Mother.

Shastri, Hari Prasad. *The Narada Sutras: The Philosophy of Love.* Translated with an introduction and commentary by Hari Prasad Shastri. London: Shanti Sadan, 1973.

Vivekananda (1863–1902). *The Yogas and Other Works.* Rev. ed. New York: Ramakrishna-Vivekananda Center, 1953. Swami Vivekananda was the principal disciple of Sri Ramakrishna and a founder of the Ramakrishna Order.

List of Special Terms □

Selected terms in Sanskrit and English are indexed here by page numbers and note numbers, directing the reader to the definition of each term.

Credits □

Thanks to the following for their kind permission to quote from published works:

Excerpts from the *Bhagavad Gita for Daily Living*, vols. 1, 2, and 3, by Eknath Easwaran, founder of the Blue Mountain Center of Meditation, copyright ©1975; reprinted by permission of Nilgiri Press, Tomales, California, www. nilgiri.org.

Excerpts from works by and about Avatar Meher Baba (including *Discourses*; *Beams*; *Listen, Humanity*; *God to Man and Man to God*; *Treasures from the Meher Baba Journals*; *The Turning of the Key*; *Lord Meher*; *That's How It Was*; and *Eighty-two Family Letters*) reprinted courtesy of the Avatar Meher Baba Perpetual Public Charitable Trust, Ahmednagar, M.S., India.

Excerpts from *God Talks with Arjuna: The Bhagavad Gita, Royal Science of God Realization*, by Paramahansa Yogananda, copyright © 1995, 1999, reprinted by permission of Self-Realization Fellowship, Los Angeles.

Commentary by Jnanadeva excerpted with permission from Swami Kripananda's *Jnaneshwar's Gita*, copyright © 1999 SYDA Foundation. All rights reserved.

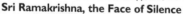
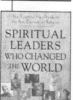
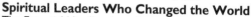

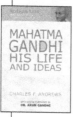

Sacred Texts—SkyLight Illuminations Series

Offers today's spiritual seeker an enjoyable entry into the great classic texts of the world's spiritual traditions. Each classic is presented in an accessible translation, with facing pages of guided commentary from experts, giving you the keys you need to understand the history, context and meaning of the text.

CHRISTIANITY

The Book of Common Prayer: A Spiritual Treasure Chest—Selections Annotated & Explained

Annotation by The Rev. Canon C. K. Robertson, PhD; Foreword by The Most Rev. Katharine Jefferts Schori; Preface by Archbishop Desmond Tutu

Makes available the riches of this spiritual treasure chest for all who are interested in deepening their life of prayer, building stronger relationships and making a difference in their world. 5½ x 8½, 208 pp, Quality PB, 978-1-59473-524-0 **$16.99**

Celtic Christian Spirituality: Essential Writings—Annotated & Explained

Annotation by Mary C. Earle; Foreword by John Philip Newell

Explores how the writings of this lively tradition embody the gospel.
5½ x 8½, 176 pp, Quality PB, 978-1-59473-302-4 **$16.99**

Desert Fathers and Mothers: Early Christian Wisdom Sayings—Annotated & Explained *Annotation by Christine Valters Paintner, PhD*

Opens up wisdom of the desert fathers and mothers for readers with no previous knowledge of Western monasticism and early Christianity.
5½ x 8½, 192 pp, Quality PB, 978-1-59473-373-4 **$16.99**

The End of Days: Essential Selections from Apocalyptic Texts—Annotated & Explained *Annotation by Robert G. Clouse, PhD*

Helps you understand the complex Christian visions of the end of the world.
5½ x 8½, 224 pp, Quality PB, 978-1-59473-170-9 **$16.99**

The Hidden Gospel of Matthew: Annotated & Explained

Translation & Annotation by Ron Miller

Discover the words and events that have the strongest connection to the historical Jesus.
5½ x 8½, 272 pp, Quality PB, 978-1-59473-038-2 **$16.99**

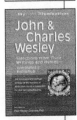

The Imitation of Christ: Selections Annotated & Explained

Annotation by Paul Wesley Chilcote, PhD; By Thomas à Kempis; Adapted from John Wesley's The Christian's Pattern

Let Jesus's example of holiness, humility and purity of heart be a companion on your own spiritual journey.
5½ x 8½, 224 pp, Quality PB, 978-1-59473-434-2 **$16.99**

The Infancy Gospels of Jesus: Apocryphal Tales from the Childhoods of Mary and Jesus—Annotated & Explained

Translation & Annotation by Stevan Davies; Foreword by A. Edward Siecienski, PhD

A startling presentation of the early lives of Mary, Jesus and other biblical figures that will amuse and surprise you. 5½ x 8½, 176 pp, Quality PB, 978-1-59473-258-4 **$16.99**

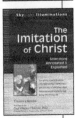

John & Charles Wesley: Selections from Their Writings and Hymns—Annotated & Explained *Annotation by Paul W. Chilcote, PhD*

A unique presentation of the writings of these two inspiring brothers brings together some of the most essential material from their large corpus of work.
5½ x 8½, 288 pp, Quality PB, 978-1-59473-309-3 **$16.99**

Julian of Norwich: Selections from *Revelations of Divine Love*—Annotated & Explained *Annotation by Mary C. Earle; Foreword by Roberta C. Bondi*

Addresses topics including the infinite nature of God, the life of prayer, God's suffering with us, the eternal and undying life of the soul, the motherhood of Jesus and the motherhood of God and more.
5½ x 8½, 224 pp, Quality PB, 978-1-59473-513-4 **$16.99**

Sacred Texts—continued

ISLAM

Ghazali on the Principles of Islamic Spirituality
Selections from *The Forty Foundations of Religion*—Annotated & Explained
Translation & Annotation by Aaron Spevack, PhD
Makes the core message of this influential spiritual master relevant to anyone seeking a balanced understanding of Islam.
5½ x 8½, 336 pp, Quality PB, 978-1-59473-284-3 **$18.99**

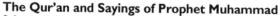

The Qur'an and Sayings of Prophet Muhammad
Selections Annotated & Explained
Annotation by Sohaib N. Sultan; Translation by Yusuf Ali, Revised by Sohaib N. Sultan; Foreword by Jane I. Smith
Presents the foundational wisdom of Islam in an easy-to-use format.
5½ x 8½, 256 pp, Quality PB, 978-1-59473-222-5 **$16.99**

Rumi and Islam: Selections from His Stories, Poems, and Discourses—
Annotated & Explained *Translation & Annotation by Ibrahim Gamard*
Focuses on Rumi's place within the Sufi tradition of Islam, providing insight into the mystical side of the religion. 5½ x 8½, 240 pp, Quality PB, 978-1-59473-002-3 **$18.99**

EASTERN RELIGIONS

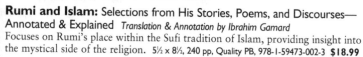

The Art of War—Spirituality for Conflict: Annotated & Explained
By Sun Tzu; Annotation by Thomas Huynh; Translation by Thomas Huynh and the Editors at Sonshi.com; Foreword by Marc Benioff; Preface by Thomas Cleary
Highlights principles that encourage a perceptive and spiritual approach to conflict.
5½ x 8½, 256 pp, Quality PB, 978-1-59473-244-7 **$16.99**

Bhagavad Gita: Annotated & Explained
Translation by Shri Purohit Swami; Annotation by Kendra Crossen Burroughs; Foreword by Andrew Harvey
Presents the classic text's teachings—with no previous knowledge of Hinduism required.
5½ x 8½, 192 pp, Quality PB, 978-1-893361-28-7 **$18.99**

Chuang-tzu: The Tao of Perfect Happiness—Selections Annotated & Explained
Translation & Annotation by Livia Kohn, PhD
Presents Taoism's central message of reverence for the "Way" of the natural world.
5½ x 8½, 240 pp, Quality PB, 978-1-59473-296-6 **$16.99**

Confucius, the *Analects*: The Path of the Sage—Selections Annotated
& Explained *Annotation by Rodney L. Taylor, PhD; Translation by James Legge, Revised by Rodney L. Taylor, PhD* Explores the ethical and spiritual meaning behind the Confucian way of learning and self-cultivation.
5½ x 8½, 192 pp, Quality PB, 978-1-59473-306-2 **$16.99**

Dhammapada: Annotated & Explained
Translation by Max Müller, revised by Jack Maguire; Annotation by Jack Maguire; Foreword by Andrew Harvey Contains all of Buddhism's key teachings, plus commentary that explains all the names, terms and references.
5½ x 8½, 160 pp, b/w photos, Quality PB, 978-1-893361-42-3 **$14.95**

Selections from the Gospel of Sri Ramakrishna: Annotated & Explained
Translation by Swami Nikhilananda; Annotation by Kendra Crossen Burroughs; Foreword by Andrew Harvey Introduces the fascinating world of the Indian mystic and the universal appeal of his message. 5½ x 8½, 240 pp, b/w photos, Quality PB, 978-1-893361-46-1 **$16.95**

Tao Te Ching: Annotated & Explained
Translation & Annotation by Derek Lin; Foreword by Lama Surya Das
Introduces an Eastern classic in an accessible, poetic and completely original way.
5½ x 8½, 208 pp, Quality PB, 978-1-59473-204-1 **$16.99**

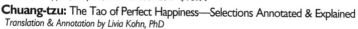

Spiritual Practice—The Sacred Art of Living

Dreaming—The Sacred Art: Incubating, Navigating & Interpreting
Sacred Dreams for Spiritual & Personal Growth
By Lori Joan Swick, PhD
This fascinating introduction to sacred dreams celebrates the dream experience
as a way to deepen spiritual awareness and as a source of self-healing. Designed
for the novice and the experienced sacred dreamer of all faith traditions, or none.
5½ x 8½, 224 pp, Quality PB, 978-1-59473-544-8 **$16.99**

Conversation—The Sacred Art: Practicing Presence in an Age of Distraction
By Diane M. Millis, PhD; Foreword by Rev. Tilden Edwards, PhD
5½ x 8½, 192 pp, Quality PB, 978-1-59473-474-8 **$16.99**

Dance—The Sacred Art: The Joy of Movement as a Spiritual Practice
By Cynthia Winton-Henry 5½ x 8½, 224 pp, Quality PB, 978-1-59473-268-3 **$16.99**

Fly-Fishing—The Sacred Art: Casting a Fly as a Spiritual Practice
*By Rabbi Eric Eisenkramer and Rev. Michael Attas, MD; Foreword by Chris Wood, CEO,
Trout Unlimited; Preface by Lori Simon, executive director, Casting for Recovery*
5½ x 8½, 160 pp, Quality PB, 978-1-59473-299-7 **$16.99**

Giving—The Sacred Art: Creating a Lifestyle of Generosity
By Lauren Tyler Wright 5½ x 8½, 208 pp, Quality PB, 978-1-59473-224-9 **$16.99**

Haiku—The Sacred Art: A Spiritual Practice in Three Lines
By Margaret D. McGee 5½ x 8½, 192 pp, Quality PB, 978-1-59473-269-0 **$16.99**

Hospitality—The Sacred Art: Discovering the Hidden Spiritual Power of
Invitation and Welcome *By Rev. Nanette Sawyer; Foreword by Rev. Dirk Ficca*
5½ x 8½, 208 pp, Quality PB, 978-1-59473-228-7 **$16.99**

Labyrinths from the Outside In, 2nd Edition: Walking to Spiritual Insight—
A Beginner's Guide *By Rev. Dr. Donna Schaper and Rev. Dr. Carole Ann Camp*
6 x 9, 208 pp, b/w illus. and photos, Quality PB, 978-1-59473-486-1 **$16.99**

***Lectio Divina*—The Sacred Art:** Transforming Words & Images into Heart-Centered Prayer
By Christine Valters Paintner, PhD 5½ x 8½, 240 pp, Quality PB, 978-1-59473-300-0 **$16.99**

Pilgrimage—The Sacred Art: Journey to the Center of the Heart
By Dr. Sheryl A. Kujawa-Holbrook 5½ x 8½, 240 pp, Quality PB, 978-1-59473-472-4 **$16.99**

Practicing the Sacred Art of Listening: A Guide to Enrich Your Relationships and
Kindle Your Spiritual Life *By Kay Lindahl* 8 x 8, 176 pp, Quality PB, 978-1-893361-85-0 **$18.99**

Recovery—The Sacred Art: The Twelve Steps as Spiritual Practice
By Rami Shapiro; Foreword by Joan Borysenko, PhD 5½ x 8½, 240 pp, Quality PB, 978-1-59473-259-1 **$16.99**

Running—The Sacred Art: Preparing to Practice *By Dr. Warren A. Kay; Foreword
by Kristin Armstrong* 5½ x 8½, 160 pp, Quality PB, 978-1-59473-227-0 **$16.99**

The Sacred Art of Chant: Preparing to Practice
By Ana Hernández 5½ x 8½, 192 pp, Quality PB, 978-1-59473-036-8 **$16.99**

The Sacred Art of Fasting: Preparing to Practice
By Thomas Ryan, CSP 5½ x 8½, 192 pp, Quality PB, 978-1-59473-078-8 **$15.99**

The Sacred Art of Forgiveness: Forgiving Ourselves and Others through God's Grace
By Marcia Ford 8 x 8, 176 pp, Quality PB, 978-1-59473-175-4 **$18.99**

The Sacred Art of Listening: Forty Reflections for Cultivating a Spiritual Practice
By Kay Lindahl; Illus. by Amy Schnapper 8 x 8, 160 pp, b/w illus., Quality PB, 978-1-893361-44-7 **$16.99**

The Sacred Art of Lovingkindness: Preparing to Practice
By Rabbi Rami Shapiro; Foreword by Marcia Ford 5½ x 8½, 176 pp, Quality PB, 978-1-59473-151-8 **$16.99**

Thanking & Blessing—The Sacred Art: Spiritual Vitality through Gratefulness
By Jay Marshall, PhD; Foreword by Philip Gulley 5½ x 8½, 176 pp, Quality PB, 978-1-59473-231-7 **$16.99**

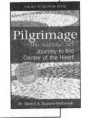

Writing—The Sacred Art: Beyond the Page to Spiritual Practice
By Rami Shapiro and Aaron Shapiro 5½ x 8½, 192 pp, Quality PB, 978-1-59473-372-7 **$16.99**

About SKYLIGHT PATHS Publishing

SkyLight Paths Publishing is creating a place where people of different spiritual traditions come together for challenge and inspiration, a place where we can help each other understand the mystery that lies at the heart of our existence.

Through spirituality, our religious beliefs are increasingly becoming a part of our lives—rather than *apart* from our lives. While many of us may be more interested than ever in spiritual growth, we may be less firmly planted in traditional religion. Yet, we do want to deepen our relationship to the sacred, to learn from our own as well as from other faith traditions, and to practice in new ways.

SkyLight Paths sees both believers and seekers as a community that increasingly transcends traditional boundaries of religion and denomination—people wanting to learn from each other, *walking together, finding the way.*

For your information and convenience, at the back of this book we have provided a list of other SkyLight Paths books you might find interesting and useful. They cover the following subjects:

Buddhism / Zen	Global Spiritual	Monasticism
Catholicism	Perspectives	Mysticism
Children's Books	Gnosticism	Poetry
Christianity	Hinduism /	Prayer
Comparative	Vedanta	Religious Etiquette
Religion	Inspiration	Retirement
Current Events	Islam / Sufism	Spiritual Biography
Earth-Based	Judaism	Spiritual Direction
Spirituality	Kabbalah	Spirituality
Enneagram	Meditation	Women's Interest
	Midrash Fiction	Worship

Or phone, mail or email to: SKYLIGHT PATHS Publishing
An imprint of Turner Publishing Company
4507 Charlotte Avenue •Suite 100 • Nashville, Tennessee 37209
Tel: (615) 255-2665 • www.skylightpaths.com
Prices subject to change.

For more information about each book, visit our website at www.skylightpaths.com

9 781893 361287